ONE
OF
THEM

MUSA OKWONGA

ONE OF THEM

AN ETON COLLEGE MEMOIR

unbound

First published in 2021

Unbound
Level 1, Devonshire House, One Mayfair Place, London W1J 8AJ
www.unbound.com

Text design by Ellipsis, Glasgow

A CIP record for this book is available from the British Library

ISBN 978-1-78352-967-4 (paperback)
ISBN 978-1-78352-968-1 (ebook)

Printed and bound in Great Britain by Clays Ltd, Elcograf S.p.A.

3 5 7 9 8 6 4 2

There are precisely two types of immigrant: those who manage to avoid detection by the most hostile forces in their society, and those who do not. This is the story of my attempt to be the former.

With gratitude to Winston Bell-Gam
for his generous support of this book

CONTENTS

PART ONE
MOSTLY PEACEFUL

JUST LIKE BEING AT SCHOOL AGAIN

One day I receive an email from an old friend, asking if I am coming to the school reunion. A few days later I receive another. *The people at school are trying to get hold of you*, they say, *but they don't know how*. I am one of about a dozen boys from my year of just over 250 students whom they refer to as 'lost leavers', those whose contact details they no longer have, and they would like to invite me to celebrate the twentieth anniversary of my departure. They've put out a list of names to all the old boys in my age group, just in case some of them are in touch with me. *Will you be coming along?* they ask. *It would be good to see you.*

I pause before replying to the email, which is always revealing: I always hesitate before delivering news people might not like. I don't want to go. A school reunion is essentially a referendum on whether I am happy to display the life I have made in front of my contemporaries, and if I am truthful with myself, then the answer is no.

My best friend from school then gets in touch. I'm not sure about this, I say to him. I could tell, he replies. He will be attending the reunion. He is a successful executive, a married father of two, with a career that has taken him across the world and back. I might feel more comfortable going back there if I was him, but I'm not; I'm a childless, unmarried writer who can't afford to buy his mother a house.

I wonder if I am being oversensitive and so I explain my doubts to another close schoolfriend, who will be attending the reunion too. I just don't feel that I have very much to show for the last twenty years, I say. That's nonsense, he says at once, but he understands my reluctance; he knows I'm not looking forward to people's judgement of my life choices. Some friends will tell me that I compare myself too harshly to my peers, but he gets it. That is precisely what my school has brought me up to do: to compete endlessly with those nearby, even as I seek my own way.

His path has been very different from mine, but he has always respected my direction. He and his wife, a couple so attractive they should be taxed for it, live with their young son in London, where they have carved out fulfilling careers in the legal profession. I try to see them at least once a year when I am back from Berlin, where I now live, but our diaries are more and more unforgiving as time goes by. I don't think I'll go.

What have I done with my life? My school asks me this every decade, whenever it has a reunion, and the last time they did so the answer was: *So far, so good.* I had published two acclaimed books about football and several of my contemporaries had read them. I was on my way to a black-tie dinner with some of the game's most celebrated players. I was running one of the most successful poetry nights in London and had made a promising start to a career in music.

Ten years later, I haven't yet published a third book about football, and I have had to publish my own poetry because no one else would. I am barely making music any more, partly because that scene has been ravaged by internet piracy, and though I am making my name as a journalist, the industry is imploding. On social media I see many friends of mine provide summaries of their last ten years and all the things they have done in that time. I don't write a summary. My best years are ahead, I tell myself. They have to be.

There's another reason I don't want to go back to school, which is that it feels like the bad guys have won. A few years before I arrived at my school, it was attended by a cluster of people who now hold political office in Britain: a group who have driven through some of the most socially regressive policies in recent memory, and whose leader, the current prime minister, is best known for his arrogance and dishonesty. I was so proud of my school when I was there, but now I wonder what kind of place it was if these are its most prominent alumni. I ask myself whether this was my school's ethos: to win at all costs; to be reckless, at best, and brutal, at worst. I look at its motto again – 'May Eton Flourish' – and I think, yes, many of our politicians have flourished, but to the vast detriment of others. Maybe we were raised to be the bad guys?

I don't think I was, but I am not so sure any more, because if I wasn't, then where is the resistance? Where are the good guys from my school who are speaking up against the bad ones? I don't see many of them arguing for a more compassionate world in the public sphere, or funding media organisations or progressive causes; not nearly on the same scale that the bad guys are. I tell a schoolfriend this and he says, Maybe they are working hard behind the scenes, and I say that even if this is happening – which I very much doubt – then it is not good enough. It is just like being at school again, I think. Just like being at school, when people would complain furiously about the few boys who ran the place, but never actually said anything to their faces.

Just like being at school again. The invitation to my reunion and the rise of another one of my school's old boys to the office of prime minister have brought me abruptly and painfully back to my teenage years. Maybe I need to stay here awhile, to see why these feelings are still so severe.

LOOKING FOR ME

Years later, a few people will look forgivingly upon those who went to Eton, saying that it is not their fault that their parents sent them there. They will say that these boys are not to blame for choosing to attend a place whose most famous alumni are now wrecking the country and causing so much anger elsewhere around the planet. I will read and hear their words and I will think: But I did choose it, and I was proud when I did so.

I remember that day well. I was eleven years old, and a documentary came on television celebrating the 550th anniversary of a world-famous boarding school. I was transfixed. Everything they did there seemed so important – the routines, the rituals. How did a simple school get to look so grand? At that time, I was attending a normal-sized school – the kind of school that only came into view once my mother's car drove over a small railway bridge. But this school I was seeing on television, it was the size of a town. Years later, when I am landing in Heathrow, I will be able to see it easily from the air and will always look for it as I descend. Sometimes I will even be able to pick out my boarding house, from which I saw countless planes come in as I worked at my desk; how many of those who studied where I did were in those planes then, looking down just as I looked up, looking for me?

This school! Two weeks later, by complete coincidence, I will visit it for a school trip, and I will get to see its majesty up close. Its bricks are five times as old as those of my home town. It has statues of kings and monuments to biblical heroes. It is part museum, part war memorial. It has several great halls and not one church but two, these vast buildings of forbidding stone and marvellous stained glass. Places of worship that God himself might attend.

I get home from my school trip and I speak to my mother that evening. I have to go to that school, I tell her. I have to. My mother is surprised by my determination, and I am even more surprised by how quickly she agrees. After all, the change will not be convenient for her. I have just won a place at the local grammar school, which I am set to attend free of charge, and now I want to go to an institution which, over the next few years, will cost her tens of thousands of pounds.

I don't think of any of that now; I am only eleven, and all that matters is reaching the destination that I now crave. There is only one thing I have been thinking since I saw that documentary: that this is the best school in the world, the home of past and future heads of state, and if I succeed there, I can succeed anywhere. It will be a long time until I realise just how great a burden that expectation is going to be.

THE SUNSET ITSELF

I have grown up in Yiewsley, a small town just outside London; a town so small that no one I meet has heard of it or the town next to it. I live in a quiet cul-de-sac at the bottom of a long road, at the top end of which was a football stadium. There, while still a small child, I could hear the chants from the ground on midweek evenings, but the chants weren't loud or plentiful enough, and the team soon left, the ground closed down. The stadium, the only rousing part of my immediate surroundings, became a shuttered husk.

Maybe this is an ideal place for refugees to come, hide away and recover. My parents fled a war in Uganda in the mid-1970s, one in which hundreds of thousands of their fellow citizens were killed; my father returned to his country a few years later to fight in the sequel to that war, where he was killed too. I was just four when that happened. My first memory of him was his coffin in his living room back in Uganda; my second memory of him was putting the first handful of dirt on his grave. My home town seems to be the perfect antidote to all of that turmoil, as do many of the equally sleepy outer reaches of London. Nothing, as I will often moan, ever happens here.

Every few days my mother will drive me over to see my grandparents, who live twenty minutes' drive away in a house my family has bought for them. They came here to escape the same bloody sequel that killed their son-in-law, to live out their days in a distracted peace. Few things are more poignant to witness than the final years of a frustrated revolutionary. They have taken the greatest gamble of their generation and lost, and are left to watch the aftermath of their heroic failure, a future that has turned out exactly as they feared and expected. The only solace they will ever have is the knowledge that they were right to act. Meanwhile, the world rolls on without them.

My grandparents resisted the emerging regime in their country, and that is why they are here now, set to perish thousands of miles from villages that they loved far more than their conquerors ever could. Those who did not resist are now widely regarded as shrewd, having made millions of dollars many times over. They have now released a fleet of autobiographies about their thrilling paths to financial success, books that contain very few sentences about the importance of doing everything in their power to keep a dictator happy.

My grandparents now live within a very small orbit. They have found great kindness and friendship at a local chapel a few streets away, and take frequent walks in the local park, which is even closer. My grandmother cooks meals that remind her of home, and my grandfather, a headmaster before the war started, has begun work on a dictionary for English speakers who wish to learn the language of my ethnic group. He spends many evenings upstairs at his desk, drafting away in his meticulous and elegant hand, each letter sharing the same perfect slant as the last.

In the evenings they sit in the living room, my grandfather in a plastic summer chair, being distrustful of soft seating. My grandmother is always closest to the hallway, and she is the first person I see whenever I enter the living room; my grandfather is always right next to the French windows, a few yards from the rose bush one of my eldest cousins is trying to grow in the back garden. That small lawn is bordered by a narrow alleyway and a tall fence, which keeps the main road from view. Growing up, my grandparents' horizon was the sunset itself, and now their horizon is no further away from them than the width of a ditch.

TO AVOID DETECTION

We are only 10 per cent, says one of my relatives. She gets anxious whenever she sees people from ethnic-minority backgrounds speaking out about racism. She is worried because ethnic minorities only make up 10 per cent of the UK's population; they are not a significant part of its social fabric. If she had it her way, they would be not seen and not heard. This is their country, she tells me. They don't like it when we talk about these things too much. We need to just keep our heads down. Like many of my family, she reminds me that, whenever possible, I must avoid detection. Look at the Chinese, she says, they keep themselves to themselves. Not like we black people.

I strongly fear that non-white people – especially black ones – do not have the option of being unseen, but in the early part of my life I will still do my best to be invisible, to avoid detection. I try to do this by having a spotless disciplinary record and seeking academic excellence. Study is my way to escape the radar, and from primary school onwards the standard is set. What mark did you get in school today? asks my mother as she drives me home. Ninety-nine, I reply. What happened to the one per cent? she asks. Again and again I score ninety-nine. Finally, I score one hundred and I can't wait to tell her the news. What mark did you get today? she asks me. One hundred, I say, my heart soaring with pride. Do it again, she says.

It's the only way I can break free of racism, my mother reminds me; by being the best. *If you're black, you need to work twice as hard to get a half of what white people get.* I do a quick calculation and realise that I have to work four times as hard as the hardest-working white people I know to get the same as they do – surely that is not possible? But then I look at my mother and realise that this is exactly what she, a doctor and a widow with five kids, is doing. She is often gone before I wake and returns after I am in bed. One winter I will accompany her to the Midlands, to wait in the car for her and keep her company as she carries out a series of house visits, and I will think, My God, this woman never stops. If she doesn't relent, then neither, under any circumstances, can I.

NO ONE SAW YOU

Before I can attend the school of my dreams, I must go to a preparatory school for two years. As its name suggests, I will need to prepare for life in a different academic system, and so in that short time I will have to learn a range of subjects I have never studied before. My mother and I look at a couple of schools and I decide upon one a few miles further into the commuter belt, a small one with just under 150 students. The headmaster assesses my potential and is kind enough to offer me a place at a third of the normal fees.

With so much work to do, I must get started at once. I go into school and say goodbye to my closest friends, which is the first time that any of them have any idea that I am leaving. I am only eleven, but I have no idea how much I will miss them. Years later I will meet with two of them for drinks in west London. I have seen them only twice in over twenty years. The moment I see them walking up the road, the old jokes begin again. Their company is an absolute delight.

After you left, there was a big gap in the class, one of them says. We came back to class for that final term and it was weird how you were just gone. You just disappeared after that. No one saw you.

I can't tell them what I want to, which is that it would have been more painful to stay in touch with them. At some point, I had decided that in order to succeed in this new environment I would need to immerse myself in it. I instinctively knew that moving too swiftly between these two worlds could rip me apart.

THE SILENCE OF HER CAR

It's time to get ready for my prep school. I go shopping with my mother for my uniform and I think, My God, so many clothes. My surname is sewn onto each item, which makes me feel strangely official. She fills a vast trunk with all my new possessions and drives me to school at the start of the summer term, heading away from the grey and beige of my suburb and into the land of sandstone pavilions and soaring trees.

Since this is the summer term, I am one of the few new students to arrive. I meet some of the other boys in the front of the school, and they are all friendly, strikingly busy, pouring through its hallways like shoals of fish. There are just over a hundred of us there, and soon enough I will know nearly everyone at least by name. I am looking forward to this new life, and the only complication is having to say goodbye to my mother.

Since I wish to avoid crying, the trick is not to look back as she leaves the room. She hugs me goodbye and as soon as she does, I turn away so that by the time she departs, my back is turned. Her car is parked near the front of the school and so I listen for the motor to start up, that sound I would recognise anywhere. She has had that car for four years now; I was with her when she bought it in south London, rolling out of the showroom on a sunny day, and this is the first time it has left me anywhere overnight. I am pretending to talk with my classmates as I hear her go, but years later the only thing I will remember of my conversation is the silence of her car at the heart of it.

THEY ARE NEVER IMPATIENT WITH ME

My first term at my preparatory school is an academic disaster. I am competing against people who have been learning Latin and Greek since they were seven, and so they have a head start of several years. I finish bottom or close to the bottom of every class and end-of-term test with the exception of English, the one subject in which there is a broadly level playing field. My history exam is a farce – I don't realise that the year 1420 is actually in the fifteenth century, and so I write about entirely the wrong century instead. My examiner gives me seven marks out of fifty, which I suspect is partly out of sympathy.

Despite my struggles in the classroom, I quickly make friends, the closest of whom always seems to be making mix-tapes of his favourite rap tunes. The most impressive boys in my school are the two who will go on to captain the football team in successive years – they are fair-minded and diligent, and everyone seems to like them. I manage to get into the school athletics team, where I compete in the long jump, and my squad turns out to be one of the best on the local circuit.

My teachers are fun too. A couple of them are men with dry senses of humour and pasts in the army. One of them is so absent-minded that one of my classmates manages to slip an item of that morning's fried breakfast into his jacket pocket as he walks past. One of them sees me punching someone who was making fun of how primitive Africans eat, an uppercut delivered at the dinner table as we both started our dessert, and he lets me off the hook. Another one has a voice so deep that its echo could cause an avalanche. They all know how much learning I have to do to catch up with the rest of the class, and they are never impatient with me.

My favourite teacher takes me for French, which for a couple of years ends up being my best subject. When he is looking for the right expression, he slowly rubs together one of his thumbs and forefingers as if trying to taste the language with them. He corrects my text as I watch, his handwriting a long, looping script, his hand so relaxed that his pen threatens to fall out of it but never does.

THE CONCEPT OF MODESTY

Where I come from, we celebrate everything. Until now I have treated every goal that I have scored in every

17

playground kickabout as if it is a last-minute winner, turning away in triumph and wailing across the yard. And so when, during cricket practice, the ball is struck by a batsman and lands in my hand, I look to my headmaster and let out a yell of pride and astonishment. My God, I think, how could I have done something so brilliant? And he says that when we achieve things like that, we don't shout about it, we just tuck the ball quietly in our pocket and carry on. The joy stops in my throat. This is my introduction to the concept of modesty, with which I will have an ambivalent relationship.

The following year I am playing cricket against a school a little further along the commuter belt, and my headmaster is the umpire again. I am standing in my favourite fielding position, quite close to the stumps, and the batsman clatters a shot towards me, the ball a mean, greased blur that sears through the air no more than three inches from the ground, so low that when I clutch it with both hands I feel the whisper of the grass against my knuckles. It is the best catch I have ever taken and I am instantly ecstatic, but then I force that euphoria down and out of sight, and when I turn to my headmaster my face is a scowl. Is that modest enough for you? I think, but he merely bursts into a silent laugh.

I LET HIM DO IT

My time at prep school is mostly peaceful, apart from my treatment by one particular boy.

I am waiting in the queue for supper, at the bottom of a short staircase just in front of the dinner hall, when someone pushes past me. I ask why he has done so, but before I have finished my sentence I am falling to the floor. The boy has crunched his right hand into a fist, the knuckle of its middle finger jutting out like a ship's prow, and he has struck me in the bridge of my nose. The punch is as swift, brutal and cruel as it is precise, and I slump to my knees. The pain is brief and intense, a twenty-second migraine, gone before I have the chance to cry. No one stops to help me, and the boy walks into the hall. No one has ever punched me before. I don't know why the boy hates me, not yet. I will never tell my mother.

A few weeks later, I am sitting in the hall, making my way through the main course of my lunch. The boy is sitting a couple of places away, just within arm's reach, which is my first mistake. Pass me the pepper, he says rudely, as if he is calling a mischievous dog to heel. His tone is not a request, it is a challenge, and I accept it. I am stronger than

I was in that supper queue, I know I am. And so I say no; I tell him to say please. He refuses. He does not speak, but with a hypnotic slowness he peels a banana, extends his right arm and crushes it into my face, forcing its slime across my eyes and cheeks, and I sit there and I let him do it, and no one stops him, no one, and by the time he has finished thirty seconds later, the mush in the ducts of my eyes has mixed with my tears, hot and fat, and I rush from that blur of a room. The room is full of teachers and students, over a hundred of them, and though I know that few of them saw what has happened, I will never forget that none of them came out of that hall after me. No one ever asks how I am. I will never tell my mother.

This isn't how I wanted it to be. I saw that famous school on television, and I came to this place to prepare myself for it, and now I am filled with a misery I cannot describe. This place is where I will first learn that I do not need people, and it is a lesson I will hold selfishly for decades. That boy made me into a monkey in that hall, a wailing ape, and for decades it will be my shame that I allowed him to do it.

The boy has almost broken me, he can tell. He just needs to go one step further, and his work will be done. I see him in classes, we share the same dressing room, we are part of the same athletics team, but I never ask why he does what he does to me, why he hates me. Maybe I am still in shock, or maybe, worse, I have immediately accepted what

20

is happening to me as proper and correct, part of the price I have to pay for this chance at the best possible education.

A few weeks later, the boy tries to break me. I am walking to a church service one Sunday morning, a couple of hours after it has finished raining heavily, and as I am about to step into the chapel, I catch sight of a familiar item lying on the sodden turf nearby. It has been left there for me to see as I approach; it is my father's Bible, its soft leather cover peeled back, its frail pages face down in the soil. The boy knows my father was killed and that this is only one of three possessions of his that I now own and treasure, along with a tweed jacket and his passport. The boy – I know it is him – must have taken it all the way from my locker upstairs and laid it there for me, in hateful wait. I don't cry, in case the boy is watching me from somewhere. I kneel, pick up my father, and take him with me into the chapel. It will be years before I tell my mother about this incident, but for now I will reflect upon it, absorb it.

I report the boy to my headmaster, in the hope that he will be disciplined, but nothing is done. Perhaps that is because the boy is seen as troubled, perhaps that is because the boy is from a very prestigious family, but nothing is done. He does not even receive so much as an afternoon of detention. If anyone is going to address this individual, it will have to be me.

MAKE MY SECONDS COUNT

At the start of my second term at prep school I go for football trials, and they go so well that I am chosen as a striker for the first team. This is one of the highlights of my life so far – I get to play on a pitch as lovingly tended as a cricket square, and several of our games will see a few dozen spectators on the sidelines, sometimes more.

My headmaster gives a simple motivational speech so powerful that I will keep turning to it for years to come. You will each be on that pitch for sixty minutes, he says, with twenty-one other players. Some of you will have the ball for no more than thirty seconds, maybe less. Make your seconds count, he tells us, and you will be fine.

The game is relentless in its intensity, as if it is being played against a backdrop of drum and bass. The pitch is surrounded by trees that are no further than six feet from the touchline, which means that the crowd of around 200 boys are almost standing on the field of play. The boys howl the name of their school for the full hour, barely stopping during half-time, while one of the students flies a model aeroplane low overhead, back and forth, its sinister buzz arriving, receding, arriving throughout the contest. We are all so terrified of making an error that even when we are attacking our opponents at a corner, we are thinking of which of their players we will mark as soon as they regain possession.

As the match, still without score, proceeds to its final moments, one of our most skilful players receives the ball. As he sprints down the right wing into my opponents' half, I rush down the middle of the pitch, waiting for the pass that always comes – he always knows where I am – and sure enough, just before a defender can reach him with an anxious lunge, he thrashes a cross high towards the far post – but he has hit it too hard, and luckily my other winger is there to head the ball in my direction, and now I am rising sharply towards it, ready to meet it with my forehead, barely able to see its outline against the searing sun—

And then the ball and I, having made the briefest contact, both float back to earth, and while I land six feet from goal, the ball drifts beyond the despairing claws of the goalkeeper and into the furthest corner of the net.

The crowd of boys descends into silence, and as I run back to the halfway line to join my teammates in celebration, all I hear beneath the steady wail of the plane is my own voice through clenched teeth, a delirious whisper of *yes, yes, yes*. We win the game by a single goal to nil, and I return to school hoping that everyone will ask me about the match so that I can tell them what I did. If there is an eleven-year-old anywhere whom sport has made happier than that, then I still haven't met them.

I THINK I AM TOO GOOD

The better my football goes, the more assured I become in my place at prep school. My work is improving too, and I am catching up with my classmates; all those extra hours of study in the holidays are paying off. A few matches into the season I am scoring for the first team at the rate of almost a goal a game, and the frequent training sessions are the highlight of my week.

Halfway through one session, where the first team is playing against the second, my headmaster blows the whistle without warning and stops the entire match. With everyone watching, he calls my surname and asks me to swap my green first-team jersey for that of a boy playing in the red of the second team. I will play for them from now on, he says. At first I think nothing of it – maybe he just wants to swap the sides around – but then I am confused as I slowly understand what is happening. I have just been humiliated – I have been dropped. But I haven't done anything wrong, I think. I have passed the ball to teammates to give them more chances, I have worked hard, I haven't been boasting, I have been well behaved. Why is my headmaster doing this to me?

One of the boys on my new team mocks me all the way back from the pitch, laughing that I'm down with the likes of him now; he carries on taunting me until we are the last two people left in the changing room; he stands too close to me and mocks me one time too many and that's when I punch him in the jaw. Later that afternoon, looking down from a third-floor window, he compliments me on the force of the strike, and we are good friends after that.

I work hard in training and score for the second eleven in my next game, but I won't play for the first team again for the rest of the season. Devastated, I ask one of my former teammates what I have done wrong, and he simply tells me, The headmaster thinks that you think you are too good.

OBSERVED, EXPOSED

Though I am always prepared for him, the boy who has bullied me does not come for me again. He does come for another victim, though. I am just about to start class when I see him going over to accost one of my friends, and so at once I am out of my chair and across the room, telling myself, You might do that to me but you are not going to do it to him, maybe he is not strong enough to take it, and I fasten the boy in a headlock so that he releases my friend and then I press his cheek slowly against the desk, keeping it there even as my teacher yells at me to sit down, waiting until the boy feels the eyes of classmates turning towards him, until he feels observed, exposed. And then I let go. I walk back to my seat and there is no trouble from him after that.

THE BEST I WILL EVER PLAY

There are three highlights to my final year. The first of them is getting a place to study at Eton, the school of my dreams, the second is getting back into my school's first football team, and the third is the success of the cricket team I play for, the school's second eleven. We go through the entire cricket season undefeated, winning six games and drawing three, and my headmaster even awards my entire team a prize each at the end of it, a small wooden plaque that I place proudly on my book-case back home.

I go to take the scholarship examination, but I know as soon as I sit the papers that I have not succeeded in earning a top award. The only test in which I do myself justice is French. The atmosphere is intimidating, the interview room cavernous, the examination room a cathedral. I succeed in gaining admission, though, and I do well enough that they give my mother a 50 per cent reduction in my school fees. When I hear my results, I am not happy so much as resolute. The hard work starts now.

My second and final football season is perhaps the best I will ever play. Mindful that my headmaster sees me as arrogant, I take care to give only the merest indication of happiness when I score. I am so focused each time I take the field and I do so well that after only five matches I am given my colours, a pair of light blue socks that I will wear from now on as a visible reward for my outstanding performances.

The school long-jump competition doesn't go so well for me. My mother is so busy working that it is hard for her to come and watch me play sport, but on the afternoon of the final she manages to make it. It is the only time she sees me compete, but I lose to a boy who is so fast that he can complete the hundred metres while barely taking a breath. I then go on to take part in the qualifying heats for the national championships, with the top two going through to the finals in the Midlands, but on the final jump I am beaten into third place. Eight years later, at university, I bump into the boy who beat me with his last attempt; he is tall, confident, even cocky, just as he was then. I like him immediately. As he walks to catch his bus, I call out his surname and school in the same style of the stadium announcer back then; he turns, smiles and gives a mock bow. Haha, I think, you bastard.

One day, while I am talking with a fellow old boy of my school, he reflects on the different paths that we took to get to the school of my dreams. You had to work so hard, he said, and get all those grades, while I was put down for this place at birth, and just had to scrape in. It is a system that first strikes me as strange, and eventually as utterly unfair – where to enter this world I had to run a thousand miles, and my friend merely had to open his front door and stroll down the lawn.

PART TWO
THE SCHOOL OF MY DREAMS

IT'S THE ACCENT

Arriving at school at the start of each term will always feel so grand, like stepping into an opera house. No one here ever tells us out loud that we Etonians are natural leaders: that is what the architecture is for. In one of the rooms, where students gather now and then, I find the mounted bust of every boy who has gone on to become the leader of the country. My boarding houses look like government buildings. My school has its own vocabulary, with grand names for seemingly every task and landmark.

There are special terms for playing fields and academic performances and acts of disobedience. If you submit work of exceptional merit, then it is Sent Up for Good, a copy of it stored in the vaults of the school library for ever. If you submit work that is utterly substandard, then you are given a Rip, with the top corner of your offending paper receiving a small tear. If you arrive notably late for class, then you must get up early and walk to a school office where you must sign the Tardy Book as punishment; if you get into more significant trouble, then while you await your sentence your name is entered on a register forebodingly named The Bill. At Eton, even your mistakes are epic, and the effect of this is to give the sense that every single thing you do truly matters. As a student here, it is therefore easy for you to conclude from your surroundings that one day you will be important too.

The greatest proof of my status is my uniform. Every single day I go to class in clothing that many men wear only once in their lives, if at all: a morning suit, identical to the clothing of a bridegroom. It consists of a black tailcoat, a black waistcoat under which I wear a white shirt with a starched collar and thin white cotton tie, a pair of black pinstriped trousers and black shoes. By the time my teens are over, I will have worn one of the smartest outfits in anyone's wardrobe hundreds of times. The effect of this is that, when I put on a business suit for work or any formal occasion, I look as relaxed as if I am wearing a pair of pyjamas.

By now my accent has changed too. The adaptation has been gradual and unforced; one day I suddenly notice that I no longer pronounce milk as *melk*. Years later I will talk to a friend of mine, a black woman who also attended private school and who is now working in a hostile corporate environment. Despite her excellence at her job, she is in no doubt as to which asset serves and protects her the most. It's the accent, she tells me, almost despairingly. It's the accent.

THE NAMES

At the start of each term, every boy gets a pocketbook containing a calendar of all the scheduled events for the months to come. The book also contains an alphabetical list of all the students in the school, and it's this section that intrigues me the most. The first few times I read it, I can't stop looking at the names.

Each boy is listed by his surname and his full set of initials. I am relieved to see that I have two middle names, which is about the average – some boys are so distinguished that they have three or even four. I will never tell anyone what my middle names are – they sound very Ugandan and I am worried that revealing them and their pronunciation, which might be strange to Western ears, will leave me open to mockery. I also see that some of the surnames are followed by letters. I will soon learn that if I gain a scholarship or other similarly prestigious award, then the abbreviation of that award will be printed after my name on all official school correspondence – on my report cards, my invitations and so on. These abbreviations represent the school's very own honours scheme, perhaps preparing us for the day when our country will bestow even greater accolades upon us, and I want my own set of them as soon as possible.

Some of the surnames in that pocketbook remind me of the names of famous companies, and then I realise that these are the families that actually founded these famous companies. There are confectioners and retailers and jewellers and industrialists and financiers. One boy will later tell me the story of how his family of merchants got started, just a little stall in a market and then another and another, five generations ago, and just look where that took us, his eyes glimmering with pride. Other boys have histories of which they are less visibly proud, their ancestors having done shameful things generations before. That boy's surname is this, I will be told, but his family's name is actually that, and they don't really want people knowing that because there is still a lot of anger about it.

Some of the surnames in the book are double-barrelled, and I have never seen this before. What I also notice is that some of these double-barrelled surnames don't have a hyphen between the first part of the surname and the second part. To me, these surnames look especially posh, because when I see a hyphen in a double-barrelled surname, it feels as if I'm being urged to say it in a hurry, whereas when I don't see a hyphen, it feels as though I am being encouraged to pause after saying the first half of the surname – perhaps to take a sip of a drink or a drag of a cigarette – then to roll all that delicious prestige around the inside of my mouth before continuing.

No one at my school has heard of my surname before I arrive. One day my art teacher pronounces my name slowly, not out of any sense of difficulty, but instead as if she is assessing it. That, she says after some thought, is a good name for a writer. I don't remember if I smiled at the time, but years later I will.

CULTURE

Each boarding house, consisting of fifty boys, is its own country, has its own culture. The youngest boys live on the bottom floor, the oldest at the top, and my classmates and I will move up one floor every year. Each house either has its own dining room or its own set of tables in the main school dining room, and it has its own set of colours, which we wear whenever we compete against each other on the field of play.

Some houses are famed for their sporting prowess; when I play against them in intramural matches, everyone seems to be a member of a school team. When they don't win a trophy, it is generally a shock. In fact, those houses are so good at sport that many suspect the housemasters partly recruit the boys on that basis. My house is not like that and rarely makes it out of the first round of any sporting competition. My housemaster is much more impressed by diligence in the classroom, which leads to a happier environment overall. In the time I am there, the scholars' house – drawn from the top fifteen boys in entrance examinations each year – somehow manages to be superb at everything athletic too. Playing football against them feels like I am having an encounter with genetically modified human beings.

At first, I am in awe of the eldest boys in my house – it is the first time I have seen anyone evolving into men before my eyes. The gap between us is only a few years, but at that point in my life it is vast, and I gaze up at them as if they are gods. Very soon I realise that they are not gods and that is when I begin to mock some of them, testing their boundaries. I don't have an older brother at home, so this dynamic is new. One of them is excellent at karate, so I know better than to go after him. Another one has the permanently threatening air of a panther unfurling himself from sleep; best to avoid him too. I try my luck a little too often with some of them, and a couple of them swiftly return me to earth with a dead arm. One of them will later reflect that I am cocky but there is always a point to my disobedience. It is one of the greatest compliments I am ever paid.

I am quietly excited when they involve me in their conversations, and they are often generous enough to do so. The boys in the year directly above me are the ones I will get to know best; they are warm towards me, and a few of them are hilarious. From my conversations with my friends in other houses, this closeness is unusual: there is generally much more deference towards boys in years above, probably too much. I have my housemaster to thank for that. There is never a sense here – as in some other houses – that the boys are in control.

My relationship with my housemaster will go through several stages. First, I find him stern, a little distant, but when I meet his family my view of him changes entirely. His wife and two children are kind, wonderful people, and I realise how much of himself he must be holding back. When he is with them, his humour is almost playful. Once I become an adult, I am grateful for the outstanding job that he did. I will truly feel that he protected us from some of the school's worst excesses, never allowing any of us to get too carried away with our egos. It is striking to see what a broad range of parents trust him with their sons.

VISIBLE EFFORT IS MOCKED

I make friends in my own year pretty well. I live a couple of doors down from someone I will quickly come to see as my best friend. What a strangely good-natured boy he is, I think. As with my housemaster, I only see him lose his temper once; that was during a football match, at a boy who was goading his central European heritage. Standing almost nose to nose with the boy, each of his pupils a small mushroom cloud, he released a roar of such astonishing volume and fury that I marvel at its ferocity even today. I swear to fucking God, he yelled, if you call me that again I swear to God I will fucking kill you. The boy never calls him that again.

My best friend is good at everything but never boasts; he is frequently teased for his remarkable work ethic, but he doesn't appear to mind that either. Visible effort is mocked at my school – the trick is to achieve without seeming to try. There is a story about one of the most brilliant students in my year: whenever someone entered his room while he was preparing for his exams, his hand would rush towards his stopwatch and remain there until the intruder left the room. He didn't wish to miss a single second of his sched-uled revision time. This story is related with faint disdain rather than admiration. The really impressive ones, I am told, are the ones who don't spend much time crouched over their books and still finish first in exams. I am told that story, I soon learn, by precisely the same people who hide just how hard they are working.

My best friend isn't nearly that extreme in his methods, but in other ways he is just as meticulous. His room is laid out with the precision of a hotel foyer, with every item carefully arranged and angled just so. He has a passion for classic cars, something he shares with his father, and he quickly turns out to be one of the best rugby players in the school. Fittingly, the position he plays is that of the blind-side flanker, whose quietly skilful work goes undervalued by all but those closest to him. The only thing for which he can really be disparaged is his hairstyle: it is a multiple series of curtains jutting forward from his scalp, resembling a trilobite, one of those marine fossils you find at a museum. So, of course, I disparage him for that. He wears the trilobite on his head for a couple of years, but then he gets rid of it for something much more sensible, and then he doesn't have anything I can attack any more. He is ahead of the curve, too: by the time we finish our third year at school, it is suddenly much cooler to be enthusiastic about doing the things that we love.

GOD BLESS AMERICA

Every Saturday night is movie night, where most of the boys in the house watch a video that has been hired earlier that week. The eldest boys have their own TV room on the top floor, so the other four years of boys crowd themselves into the common room. The movie is normally a generic

Hollywood blockbuster, where each director seems to have left gaps between the dialogue long enough to accommodate the sarcastic ongoing commentary by teenage boys.

The boys in the second-highest year take the biggest table in the common room, place it sideways a few metres from the television and then put their chairs upon it, where they will watch the movie from this raised platform. I and the other younger boys sit along the walls; my favourite spot for years, until I am old enough to sit on the main table, is to the left of the room, just behind the pool table. This is the best place from which I can deliver my jokes and loudly consume my snacks. The most memorable moment of movie night comes when we are watching *Independence Day* and see the American president give a rousing speech against a set of alien invaders – no sooner has he finished his address than several of us are on our feet, beating our chests with our fists and laughing at what we see as his undignified and overblown patriotism, a few of us yelling, *God bless America*.

WHAT I LOVE ABOUT IT

Like a professional footballer who is secretly unsure that he is worth the transfer money, I am constantly aware of the high cost of my school fees. At the start of each term, I divide the sum that my mother is paying by the number of school days in the term. I work out that for every day I am there, my mother is paying about £20, and so I have to find a way of justifying that outlay. Every morning I open my diary and work out a list of productive activities. I will eventually apply to, and end up leading, every suitable society I can think of – the law society, the debating society, the school assembly committee.

What strikes me most about this place – at best, what I love about it – is just how much the teachers trust me. By the end of my time there, I will have edited every single school magazine that I can, been in charge of each group that I wanted to, had the closest thing I can to work experience. My days are a blur of budgets and deadlines, and it is utterly exhilarating. My school is essentially a youth club with apparently boundless resources. I take an extra subject, partly so I won't get bored, and I learn a lesson then that I will occasionally forget – that I am at my very happiest when I am busy, on the brink of being chaotic. The school has the same quality that will later make me fall in love with several major cities, which is that it is bottomless; I can lose myself in it. For most of those early terms I am a blur, solemnly immersed in my work.

My brains are always being tested. For the first three years at school, my year's intake of almost 260 boys will be divided into classes of up to twenty for every subject that I study, and we will be ranked every two weeks from first to last. Every two terms I will sit a series of examinations in which the top thirty-two boys in each year will be awarded distinctions, and if I achieve three distinctions in a row, then I will receive the right to call myself a scholar.

These challenges to my intellect are thrilling and constant. They remind me of those times in the holidays when my mother would give me and my siblings regular arithmetic and spelling tests, my mind feeling like it had been in the gym; it takes me back to those days at preparatory school when I would keep a dictionary by my bedside, trying to learn a few new words each day. In my first term, I finish sixteenth; two terms later, I finish twenty-first.

FATED TO BE TOGETHER

I attend class with a briefcase. I am not sure if any other school student I have ever known has attended class with a briefcase, but I do it all the same. Since I am doing very serious work every day, it seems perfectly natural. The first time I open it to place my books in there, it smells like the interior of a new car. No one ever seems to mock me for carrying one of these things around – they are probably too busy coping with the fact that they are dressed like wedding guests.

The briefcase is large, and rarely more than half full – in practical terms, a satchel might have made more sense, but there is something reassuringly heavy about this item. It feels like a companion. Since I will not have a major growth spurt until my mid-teens, it sometimes seems to be almost half my height.

Even though I probably live closer to home than anyone else at school, I suspect I go home the least. During term time, some students go home every weekend, while I do so only twice in five years: after all, I need to focus. I approach my time at school with a sense of destiny. Perhaps that is because, although this institution is more than 500 years older than me, we share the same birthday. Maybe I feel that we were fated to be together.

IN THE PRESENCE OF GREATNESS

From the way some boys play football, it is unsurprising to see what they go on to do for a living. At those trials in my first term, there is one midfielder who stands out. He is not fast, but he never stops running, nor does he fall behind the tempo of the play; though highly skilled, he is not extravagant in his use of the ball, and he never seems to misplace a pass. He is the most gifted of minimalists: a guitarist who can play the most complex of solos but confines himself to only a handful of chords, because that is what the band needs. I watch him play dozens of games in my five years there, and I only see him play poorly once. How, I ask myself, can he be that good? He goes on to manage assets with a similar precision.

My first team's goalkeeper is a future insurance broker, his voice an imposing baritone that easily carries the length of the field. The most stylish player at my trials is another goalkeeper. Even his name has a flourish; its syllables sound musical, as if he were the lead character in a Shakespearean play. When he moves across goal to save the ball, he doesn't merely dive, he soars, dismissing the ball with a flick of the wrist. I am told that he was a rugby star at his previous school and that, even though he normally kicks with his right foot, he once won a game with a left-footed drop goal. His blond hair is permanently flowing, as if it is being lightly ruffled by a wind no one else can sense. Naturally, he goes on to become a professional chef.

To my regret, I never play well enough to be selected for the school's first team's football tour. A couple of friends who do go along tell me of one memorable trip where they got to play opposition from Monaco and

Italy, winning one game and losing a couple of others heavily, but where, even in the latter case, they were in the presence of greatness. At one point, my friend said, they scored five goals in a matter of minutes, and at half-time one of their substitutes was walking around with a football balanced on his head. That substitute would come on and score shortly after his introduction, one of thirteen strikes that would enter my school's net without reply. My God, I think, but we sent a really good side out there. Their opponents must have been brutal. A few weeks later, I will be watching on television as Manchester United play against Juventus in the Champions League, and among those players listed as a reserve for the Italians, I think I recognise the surname of one of the players from that thrashing of my school. He doesn't make it off the bench.

'THE LADS'

There is a way some boys look at me here that I have never seen before. When I annoy someone in my home town, they make eye contact with me, the fury glistens in their gaze. But at Eton, if I confront one of the more arrogant students who dislikes me, there is a very particular stare they give me: a glazed expression, never fully focused, as if they are peering out into the yard at a distant and mildly irritating disturbance, a fox howling somewhere in the dark. Boys who look at me like this belong to a class that everyone refers to behind their backs as 'the lads', and they seem exempt from generally accepted codes of behaviour.

The lads intrigue me from the moment I arrive at school. There seem to be between fifteen and twenty of them in each year, and they are significantly more confident than everyone else. A handful of them have a level of self-assurance which, whenever I am within their radius, greets me with the force of a stiff breeze. The key thing with the lads is that they are impervious to peer pressure and would apparently be as comfortable with having no friends at all as with having 200. They are fascinating because they seem to defy all social conventions – I have been told my entire life that it is important to get on with people in order to succeed, but these peers of mine often seem supremely disinterested in that.

The lads have one thing in common: many of those closest to them to spend much of their time complaining about them in private but never say anything to their faces, as if they are afraid of being cast out of the golden enclosure. One of the lads is so loathed that during a cricket practice a stray ball hits him hard in the middle of the back, and while he is doubled over in pain one teacher remarks to the other, You wouldn't want that to happen to anyone, but if it had to happen to someone, it would be him.

My school never creates the lads – they arrive there with the core of their egos fully formed – but it frequently seems to end up rewarding them with some of the most senior positions in the student body. The boy who is hit with the cricket ball does not go on to become notably nicer, but he does end up as a school prefect. The lads have long ago worked out, or been told, that what matters is not being good-natured but achieving high office. In a system where boys are raised to be deferential to those in authority, they know that if they merely gain prestige, then personal popularity will follow.

The school's power structure is strange to me. The school prefects are not appointed by staff, or elected via secret ballot by their own year, both of which systems would seem far more reasonable. Instead they are chosen by the prefects in the year above. The result is that if a boy wishes to be socially prominent at school, there are only twenty people in the school whose approval he truly needs.

I watch boys campaign for election as prefects with a vigour that I will later see in the world of politics, and I will realise that this is the kind of place where these politicians learned it, that this is what they mean by networking. Networking is the art of laughing a little longer and louder than necessary at the jokes of the person whose patronage you seek, of standing silently by their shoulders when they are making a nonsensical argument, of hanging around just in case they need an extra pint, of strategically making sure you are in the same place as them on holiday. It is the least dignified behaviour I can imagine, but I will see boys carry it out with such ease that it appears to be genetic.

I think a great deal about the English concept of fair play: the idea that there are some things that are simply not done. The older I get, the more I wonder how much that concept was created to keep people of a certain social class in their place. I look at the most confident people in my year and I realise that the greatest gift that has been bestowed upon them is that of shamelessness. Shamelessness is the superpower of a certain section of the English upper classes. While so many other people in the country are hamstrung by the deference and social embarrassment they have been taught since birth, the upper classes calmly parade on through the streets and boardrooms to claim the spoils. They don't learn shamelessness at Eton, but this is where they perfect it.

JUST CONSTANTLY EATING

I have always liked eating sweet things, but now I have been unleashed. At my previous school I could only buy sweets once a week, having to queue up for them on a Sunday afternoon, but now I can buy them virtually all the time. What's more, I even have a school tuck shop, a whole establishment dedicated to the art of tooth decay. The smell of sugar surges into my nostrils as soon as I walk through the door. I generally pick up a bag of twenty or thirty sweets on the way to lessons – a mix of pink shrimps and pale green apple chews. The tuck shop also does an excellent line in sausage rolls and bacon rolls, which I indulge in when I have more time on my hands.

The legacy of the tuck shop is that I am always scoffing something or other, a habit that continues long into my adult years. One afternoon, in my early days as a trainee solicitor in London, I am making my way through yet another snack when I am stopped by a tiny gasp of horror from my supervisor. My God, she says, I have never met someone who is just constantly eating.

A SET OF DREADLOCKS

My attitude to being black at school is ultimately a simple one: since there are very few black boys there, I am more likely to get noticed, whatever I do, and so I should take special care not to get into trouble. As an adult, I will consistently be incredulous when people approach me in mostly white environments and ask me for drugs. Why would I, I will occasionally ask them, when sticking out as much as this, do something so obviously criminal?

Several of my white peers have the luxury of being indistinguishable from each other from a certain distance, and they exploit this gift when fleeing from the school's authorities. One of my peers, though white, does not enjoy this anonymity: when he sprints, his buttocks look like two men fighting to push past each other on an escalator. It is a unique running style and one that would immediately identify him to police. I hope for his sake that he never gets into trouble, but he does.

There are a handful of other black and biracial boys at school in the time I am there. When I arrive, there is one who strolls everywhere as if the street beneath his feet were a red carpet. He is from a family that is prominent on the political scene in East Africa. There is another one, from the same kind of background as me, who tries all the haircuts that I wish that I had the guts to: an Afro, a set of dreadlocks. I don't dare attempt anything that eye-catching. For one thing, I already stand out enough as it is, and for another thing, I don't have the diligence for the effort required. That Afro, in particular, looks like a nightmare to maintain. Every morning it floats carefree above my friend's scalp, as if it magically stayed aloft overnight, but I know that thing needs loving revival each day.

My relationship with my hair is far more distant, and the only time I think of it is with sheer terror when I see an older black woman in town and I realise that I haven't brushed it. In that moment, every such woman becomes a disapproving aunt, the look of disappointment searing from their eyes and shuddering along the entire coastline of their jaws. Inside, I almost find myself apologising, I am sorry Auntie, and sometimes my hand moves up towards my forehead, and to cover my embarrassment it forms a temporary hat. I can never tell if you have done your hair or not, says one of my white schoolfriends, at which I grimace and reply, Just trust me, black people can tell all right.

THE COMMON PEOPLE

They call them lebs. That's the word several of my classmates use to describe the locals, taken from the Latin word *plebs*, the common people. It is a word those classmates only use among themselves, mainly because it might be risky to show such prejudice to the faces of those who are the subject of it. I hate this word at once because I know they are talking about my friends from back home. It will not be until years later that they discover the word chavs, which has been made popular by some of the nation's most beloved comedy shows, and realise to their glee and relief that much of the rest of the country is laughing at poor people too. I will go on to hate that word as well.

During the school term my encounters with local people are fairly rare. Most of them happen on the football field, against the rival boys' school, where the contests are predictably intense. One year, after a choice series of comments about one of the opposition players, one of my teammates gets his nose broken.

It is odd, having grown up in a nearby area, to now be the target of class-related aggression from those in the same area, but that is not exactly a case I can plead when high, hard and late challenges are flying at me. These matches are mostly fair, and mostly good games to watch, conducted in a largely humorous spirit. On one occasion, upon missing an excellent chance, I am loudly informed by a parent on the sideline that I could not even score with a penis.

A few minutes later, in the same match, I run onto a through-ball, pursued by the same defender with whom I had been playing games of five-a-side football for the whole of the previous summer. Over that time I had established a rapport with him, perhaps even the beginnings of a friendship. As their goalkeeper advances from his line, I extend my right foot to lob the ball over him; and then my new friend chooses that moment to clatter me with a tackle from the side, masterfully masking the fact that he has made no contact with the ball, leaving the posh boy sprawling in agony in the mud. He grins as he jogs away. I grimace, and I don't play again for three weeks.

WHAT ELSE BRITAIN DID

One of my favourite subjects is history, and it is here that I learn something that I will quote in quite a few articles and other arguments of mine over the coming decades, and which inspires me in several of my attempts at activism. The lesson comes in the form of bright-red writing across an essay of mine, my analysis of the beginning of the Second World War, in which I stated that there was a point after which that conflict became inevitable. *Nothing in history,* writes my teacher in a sprawling script, *is inevitable, only increasingly probable.* I don't love the mark he deservedly gives me for my efforts – a meagre fourteen marks out of twenty-five – but I do love what he has told me. I take from it a reminder that I should never give up, that no political cause is lost, that there is always hope of a better world.

Given the importance of history, I find it interesting to reflect on what I was taught about Britain at school, as well as what I wasn't. Upon leaving, if someone had asked me what I knew about the British Empire, I would probably have told them that the country of my birth had long ruled the world through a heady mix of commerce and conquest. Had I been asked about the details of that conquest, my answers would have been uncertain. I wouldn't have been able to tell them much, if anything, about Partition or the Opium Wars or the scramble for Africa or the trade of enslaved people, because I covered those pivotal historical events in little or no depth. I therefore grew up with a somewhat hazy sense of the British Empire; it was an edifice as distant, grand and unknowable to me as the statues of Easter Island. The conflict in Uganda was already so protracted that there was little discussion of the colonial power that had destabilised my parents' country long before and given it its present-day form. But Britain's imperial machinations were never lost on my grandfather, who once told me in an ominous tone – one that demanded no further clarification – *The last man on Earth will be an Englishman.*

It is not as if I am not taught much about Britain. I learn about when Julius Caesar and William the Conqueror invaded the island and about when its barons forced the king to submit with the Magna Carta. I learn about its struggle to resist the influence of the Continent, its stand-off with the Vatican. I spend far more time studying Britain's role in the end of slavery than its prominent role in promoting and profiting from this uniquely lucrative system of human suffering. In my view, my country was primarily the great liberator, not the cruel subjugator. I could reel off all kinds of facts about how terrifying the Vikings were, but if someone had asserted that the British could be similarly barbaric and on a far greater scale, then at first I might have been very defensive.

The Britain about which I learn is either heroic abroad or beset by internal turbulence or doing its very best to repel external threats. My Britain is a victim and yet somehow ruling and never being enslaved; it is being free and then breaking further free; a plucky underdog or the victor of fair fights; a reluctant and dignified winner of the rough and tumble of global politics. My Britain is quiet and unassuming, yet somehow stumbled upon the possession of all this territory abroad, a bumbling traveller who wandered about the world and just happened to come home with the lion's share of its wealth.

The only time I examine the sustained savagery of which Britain has been capable is during one of my specialist subjects in my final year. Here I look at the First Crusade, whose harrowing climax – the slaughter of Jews and Muslims by Christians at the siege of Jerusalem – fundamentally reshapes the way in which I look at the Middle East. I begin to see that Britain is not an innocent actor in so many of these scenarios but a much more sophisticated player than I ever imagined.

It will still be a few years until I find out about what else Britain did – about the Amritsar massacre and the Bengal famine and the eviction of the people of the Chagos Islands and the suppression of the Mau Mau, many of whose resistance of British rule was punished by their castration with pliers. It will be even longer until I learn about Operation Legacy, the British government's carefully orchestrated destruction of the bulk of the records of what it did in colonial times, so that the countries recently released from its rule would not know the extent of its deeds. I will wonder then why a country that proclaims itself to be so proud of the tale of its past has committed such huge resources to erasing so many of its chapters.

The stories of what else Britain did are all around me at school, displayed in plain sight. They are the stories behind the surnames of so many of my contemporaries. They are the stories behind so many of the busts I see in that grand room, behind the figures of many of the prime ministers who once attended my school. But I don't talk about them. I am instead raised to revere the mere fact that these men were pre-eminent, even dominant, without being asked to assess or question what they did with that power.

A friend of mine will jokingly ask on social media how the British, given their seeming inability to communicate directly – hiding so many of their questions and advances in shyness and social awkwardness – managed to conquer so much of the planet. I will reply that this is exactly how they did it; that this apparent bashfulness hides a ferociously competitive spirit. I will eventually understand that when it comes to avoiding detection, shielding its true nature from the world, no one has ever been better at it than the British Empire.

A FOOD FIGHT

I get caught causing trouble in the lunch hall. One morning I am finishing my breakfast when a friend of mine, a boy from another house, throws a cherry at me. I laugh, pick it up and throw it back, and all of a sudden one of the staff is standing at the end of the table. He tells me that he saw the whole thing and he demands our names.

The whole thing? But it was just—

We are reported to our respective housemasters, who are upset at the news that we were found having a food fight.

A food fight? It was a cherry, I think, but the image in my housemaster's mind is probably horrific, having been amplified by the staff member who reported me.

The punishment procedure is terrifyingly thorough: I am registered as an offender; a stern look and verdict are delivered. I won't feel this bad again until I am a student in my early twenties, when a bailiff pursues me for £50 of council tax as if I had stolen his inheritance. The bailiff is only called off when he realises that he is coming after me by mistake, but that is only after he has sent several aggressive letters and made promises to visit my house.

I receive my punishment – a week emptying the food from the kitchens – and I don't throw anything in the lunch hall after that. That is the only major blemish on my behavioural record in all my time at school, for one simple reason: that while the prospect of cleaning out the bins is a powerful deterrent, it was nothing compared to the dread of my mother finding out.

OH, HE'S ONE OF THEM

In my home town I reach an age when the police begin to see me, and it does not come with a warning. For much of my early life I will happily approach them in the street to ask for directions, and then at one point in my teens my relationship with them abruptly changes.

My mother has given me her bank card so I can take out some money for her for that afternoon's shopping, and so I walk along to the local bank on the high street. The cashpoint is out of order and the bank branch is shut, so I walk over to the copy centre to print out a short story I have been working on. Upon leaving the copy centre, I catch sight of the police, who have just arrived in the forecourt, and they make eye contact with me.

You there, they say. I stop, turn and walk over to them. Can I help? I say. There's been a robbery in the area, they tell me, and the suspect is someone with my description. Me, I think, a stumbling, awkward teenager who would come off badly if accosted by a mild breeze? But I haven't done anything, I say, I was just trying to get some money out of the bank for my mum. Come over to the car please, they say. They make me put my palms on the roof of their vehicle and my jacket falls open, making it easier for them to search my pockets. They take out my mother's bank card. They are parked next to the main road and so people are going past the scene on foot and in their cars, and when I catch their gaze, I see that expression on their faces: *Oh, he's one of them.*

The police let me go and I am only a few metres from my front door when I realise that I am shivering as if I have a light fever. My mother opens the door and my voice is suddenly hoarse as I tell her what has happened, and though I am thirteen I feel as if I am ten, crying as I speak. Tears have a particular heat when they are wept out of shame; I can almost see the steam rising from them as they descend across my cheeks, and my head is lowered as I look at my mother through their glaze. I stand there as she calls the police station and tells them how upset I am, and they tell her that they were just doing their job. They will always just be doing their jobs, but it is interesting that none of my close white friends at home or at school ever seem to have similar experiences, even though over the years several of them will be far more familiar with illegal acts than I ever will.

A LARGE BOWL OF COCAINE

My school is so tough on the use of drugs that I am amazed anyone would take them on school grounds. One person I know is found in possession of weed one morning and he is gone by the afternoon, without even a chance to say goodbye to his friends. I never see him again. Despite his expulsion, there is no shortage of my contemporaries who take drugs, but they keep it strictly to themselves. I am especially strait-laced and will not touch so much as a drop of alcohol until I have left university.

My reasons for being so are two-fold. First, looking around my school, I think it is unlikely that many, if any, of my contemporaries have had a close black friend, and so I don't want to conform to any of the stereotypes they might have about black people. I resolve never to get drunk around any of them, never to get stoned in their company. I don't even risk getting a haircut that I might enjoy. Even though I conduct myself with a military level of self-restraint, it is unclear whether my classmates either notice or care.

The second reason that I do not touch drugs is because I am neither white nor from the types of social networks that would give me a second chance if I was expelled. I don't have that luxury. If I was caught with weed and kicked out, I would forever be the black guy who had it all and blew it. Unlike some of my fellow students, I do not have another home on another continent where I could lie low for a few years while the controversy blew over. I am not bitter about that; I merely have to remind myself not to get too comfortable in this world. It is not my own and its rules do not apply to me.

I speak to one close black friend, from the same sort of social background as me, who tells me about a party they attended with some rich white friends of theirs. My friend tells me that, in one of the rooms, they saw a large bowl of cocaine in the middle of one of the tables. What the hell! I exclaim. What did you do when you saw it? I didn't take any, says my friend. That's not the point, I say, you should have left the party as soon as you laid eyes on that thing. If the police ever turned up at a place like that, all my friends would be able to pull out their lawyers before I could blink. Their parents probably have the kinds of connections that could get them out of trouble at once. One of them is probably the son of a judge. But you and me, we can't do that. If the police walk into a place like that, they're going to look around at all those rich kids and then, if anything, they're going to pin that on someone like us, and suddenly that bowl of cocaine becomes ours. You understand? My friend nods, now suitably chastened. They understand.

THE REAL WORLD

If you want to get to London by train from Eton, then there are two ways you can do it. The first route is by walking over the bridge and turning up the hill past the castle to one of the two stations in the neighbouring town; you then take that train one stop and change for the express that takes you to the north-west of the city. The second is by walking over that same bridge and turning left at the foot of the hill, and then almost imme- diately you'll be at the other station, which takes you directly to London's south-west. The former route rushes you through the front seat of the suburban commuter belt, and the latter route is glorious. It takes you through the sleepy backstreets of the Thames Valley and a succession of riverside villages, then on through the midst of understated wealth until arriving at the central terminal. You never have to set foot in your surroundings: at best, you can glimpse them from the window.

Over the years I will think about that second route a lot, that umbilical cord that funnels boys directly from school to their homes. People often ask how it is possible to remain out of touch with the majority of society for your entire life, but it's really quite simple. If you go to a preparatory school from the age of seven, then you board at Eton till eighteen, then you live with your schoolfriends in private accommodation at university, and then you see them all in the City, you essentially spend your formative years in a gated community. That's why you see politicians who attended boarding school looking bewildered when they wander around underfunded areas of the country – it's because they are seeing actual poverty for the first time.

As my time at school comes to an end, I will hear people talking about where they will go on their gap year: that is to say, the twelve months that many students will spend abroad before going to university. During these discussions, they will refer to the Real World in capitals, as if it were a foreign country – which, in a way, I suppose it is. It isn't very kind of me, but I will overhear these conversations and think, You don't need to go to India to find yourself; you'll learn more about life by getting off the train twenty minutes from your own house.

The older I get, though, the more I will understand it. How else would I break free, even if temporarily, from an atmosphere that so comprehensively defined me? I remember the story of a boy who spent part of his gap year trekking across a continent, armed with little more than a rucksack and his father's credit card. He'd make his way from town to town, and then when he'd tired of taking too arduous a path, he would check into one of the finest hotels he could find. In a funny kind of way, I respect that. He knew his limits; he understood that he wasn't an intrepid adventurer, that wherever he went he would always have a taste for comfort, for luxury. He was an extreme example, though. Plenty of other boys did summer jobs for a few months then disappeared to the other side of the world for some time, returning with perfect tans.

I never consider taking a gap year because that would mean relaxing, and I am several years from being able to do that. What people do not realise is that when you are the child of refugees you very often collect the baton from your parents and simply continue running. The main lesson that I have taken from my mother's successful escape is that constant work is the key to survival. Even though I am now living in a country that has not seen a civil war for centuries, there is a quiet reminder buried beneath every long-term strategic decision that I take, and it is this: remember that there is a day when you will have to run.

I don't envy my friends many things, but I do envy them their sense of comfort, their understanding that everything is going to be okay. In time, I will understand that this sense is not so lightly held, that it is something of an illusion, that working hard to have the same things as everyone around you creates its own brutal pressure. But that time will not come for a long while, and I am not yet happy enough within myself to appreciate my own freedom.

BLACK PEOPLE'S MEREST MOVEMENTS

The police ask what I am doing in the area. I smile at first and almost laugh, but I then realise what I am truly doing in the area, which is that I am being too tall and too dark and too teenaged. So I answer, I live here. Where? they ask, but I know that they are not entitled to that precise information. Up near the main road, I say, I've been here my whole life.

The police, a white man and a white woman, have approached me at a bus stop as I and two male cousins are about to head into the larger nearby town. They haven't asked anyone else what they are doing here, an elderly white man and a young white man, slightly older than me. What are you up to today? they ask, and my cousins just shake their heads, less afraid to show disdain. They are visiting from a country where police often respond to black people's merest movements with lethal force, and so for them this interaction must feel like a holiday. Years later I will remember that I was really looking forward to whatever I had planned to do that afternoon, but the only thing I now recall is meeting the police.

I think of all the times that me and my family and our friends were interrupted just for being black, and how much happier we'd be if we were just allowed to proceed. I think of all the spontaneous joy that we might have found up ahead, the days out that would have remained untainted by moments like this, these interventions that were intended to put us in our place. One reason I worked so hard at school was so that maybe one day I would be able to escape interruptions like this, but I realised in time that I was naive, that as a black person these limits on your freedom always find you.

SURELY IS NOT A QUESTION

Does anyone have any questions? asks my teacher.

Yes, says one of my classmates, leaning dangerously far

back in his seat and clutching at the air as if it were a handrail on a swerving train. My teacher nods for him to proceed.

Surely, Sir, the—

As my classmate continues to speak, my teacher looks at him in bemusement.

Where's the question? my teacher asks.

Flustered, my classmate repeats himself.

Surely, Sir, the—

No, says my teacher. Any sentence that begins with surely is not a question.

Ah, says my classmate, and asks a question instead.

My teachers are continually testing us, eternally sparring with those boys who think they have sharper wits. I never forget anything they say when they admonish me, often remembering their criticisms word for word. Following one stage of a school debating contest, having watched me and my teammate defeat an opponent, my teacher calls me over. You didn't need to do that, he says. At some points you were mean today. I am taken aback by this, not because I think it is untrue, but because I suspected I was being too harsh in my manner, that I was aware that my tongue could wound and didn't mind if it did. I take note of this, and I try to make sure not to do it again. I don't need to win that way.

HOW AFRAID I WAS

I have travelled with my classmates to see a new production of a Shakespeare play. The theatre is about three hours away by coach, in a town so small that when I leave the auditorium at 9 p.m. all the fast-food outlets are shut. Furiously hungry, I board the bus home. A good way into the return trip, someone has the idea of doing a collection for the driver, to give him a tip as a thank you for taking everyone on such a long journey. An envelope is slowly passed down the bus, and boys plunge their hands into their pockets, reaching for change or even notes. As the envelope comes to the row just before me, one of the older boys seizes it and tips it to one side so that the coins slide to that corner and form a bulge. He examines this swelling for a moment, then begins to empty the contents of the envelope into the pocket of his jacket.

Hey, what are you doing? I ask. The boy ignores me at first, his sneer fading in and out of the dim lights. I ask again and he looks at me briefly, then away, perhaps for backup. Another boy walks towards the back of the bus, towards where I am sitting. He takes the stance that boys

68

like him adopt when addressing an inferior life form, angling his head backwards as far as he can, as if he wishes me to stare all the way up his nostrils and into the beginnings of his brain. From that majestic height, he peers at me and produces his verdict on me. Typical second year, he proclaims, and calls me arrogant. Fair enough, I think. But my challenge has been successful. His friend, his expression even surlier than before, removes the coins from his pocket and returns them to the envelope, which he hands back down the coach. My best friend, sitting next to me, has seen the whole thing. That was brave, he says. I look out of the window so no one can sense how afraid I was.

I'M STILL TRAVELLING

I have started playing basketball, but I am not yet tall or quick enough to be good at it. I turn up at the gym each week and the best player there is a point guard who talks even faster than he passes, slinging assists and swear words in the direction of any teammate brave enough to catch either. He is intense as a bonfire, ripping through a forest of bodies on his way to the rim, the trail of his rage echoing off the dull green walls of the court. He likes me.

The first few times I play with him I wait for him to make eye contact before he gives me the ball, which is a grim mistake, because he never does. Instead, he seems to toss it at me when I am least prepared.

The second-best player there, by a narrow margin, is a boy in my boarding house. It seems that each time I try to shoot over him, he gathers my attempt with the ease of a mosquito net catching leaves. I eventually learn that the only way to score when marked by him is to lean sharply backwards in the same instant that I jump to shoot, sending the ball on such a high arc that it almost disappears from my line of sight, hurling it to the only parts of the sky he can't reach. Years later, having grown by then and playing against shorter players, I will still lurch backwards in the act of shooting, a reflex from the days when that boy used to stuff the ball back down my throat.

The basketball team is where I'll meet some of the most inspiring and most diverse students to come through the school, who've been awarded scholarships as among the best in their respective countries. One of them is a smooth-shooting business genius from Eastern Europe, the other a point guard from East Asia with the hang time of a helicopter. Long into my thirties, I'll find myself checking on their progress, seeing what they've done with their world-changing talents. One of them is an entrepreneur, the other an executive; while they seem to have reached their destinations, I am still travelling.

A GOOD FRIEND

A good friend of mine sees me frowning one day, and he asks me what the matter is. I am wary of answering at first, but I am so grateful that someone has asked that I tell him the entire truth. Sometimes, I say, it is just very hard being black here. Just feeling so exposed, so visible. Oh, for God's sake, he says, slightly exasperated, it can't be that hard, swatting aside a sentence it has taken me months to express as if it were merely a bad debating point. He is the same friend whose father is suspicious about my presence at the school, and who has previously theorised that I might be a spy for some foreign government. This boy's father, a prominent public figure, thinks it is likelier that I have been planted there by an alien entity than that I simply passed a difficult set of exams. It is literally unthinkable to him that a middle-class black boy could arrive quite naturally at a place like this. There had to be some catch. I don't talk about race with this boy ever again – or, for that matter, about much else.

I look across the road, having heard someone call my name, and it is the unmistakable tone of a good friend.

We are fans of the same music, so we often hang out together; we have played football together and we regard each other with a great deal of affection. Can I call you nigger, he asks, like in the music? He shouts the word over the mild traffic, as if he is hurling a pass across a crowded basketball court. No, I reply, and continue walking.

One day I am minding my own business when a classmate seeks me out. He is someone who is always a little wary of me, who is not sure how to handle me. That is his problem, in fact, that he thinks I should be handled, like a creature who might leap at you the moment you open their cage.

It is easy for you, he says, whenever someone argues with you about anything, you can simply win the argument by saying they are racist.

At first, I am baffled as to what could have prompted this. Wait, I say, that's not how arguments work. You actually have to find no flaws in my logic for me to win an argument. I can't just say that I'm black and that's the end of it.

My classmate seems confused, so much so that, ironically enough, the conversation ends there. He goes on to become a director at a large investment firm. I wonder where he learned a view like that. I wonder if he is still terrified at the prospect of a black person who might disagree with him, and whether he will treat that disagreement as an accusation of racism.

PRETTY STRONG VIEWS

I have learned from the King James Bible to associate homosexuality with weakness, and anyone who appears weak, who does not have the door to their emotions firmly welded shut, must therefore be homosexual. I argue with a boy one day, a gentle soul, and I call him gay and I see his shoulders flinch. My God, I think, this word has power.

I have learned this power over time. I have begun to understand from Christianity that this thing is an abomination: it says so clearly in the book. One day, when I am coming out of my boarding house, I make a homophobic remark within earshot of a good friend of mine. He turns to me, his eyes seething. One of my best friends is gay, he tells me. Oh, I say. I don't know what else to say at first, and then I apologise to him. I am fourteen and until this moment I have never known of a gay person. Homosexuality is an abstraction, a distant threat, a shadowy figure I will never encounter, and all of a sudden it is utterly close. Using the word gay as an insult had become a habit, a thing I would casually throw into conversation, but now I am seeing its terrible human cost. Startled, ashamed, I bow my head and stumble on with the rest of my morning.

Yet it still takes me a while to turn away from this prejudice. A few months later I bump into one of my favourite teachers. He is in his late twenties and already seems to have been on three lifetimes' worth of adventures. If I had to write a list of people I revered in this place, then he would be in the top three. Hey, he says. Pretty strong views about homosexuality you've got there. He is referring to a remark I made about homosexuality in a recent debate, where I effectively regurgitated the contents of Leviticus.

My God, I think, he sounds so disappointed. He doesn't look offended, or angry, he just seems to have thought that I was much better than that. I begin to talk about what religion has taught me but then I stop and listen to him, hearing him out. If someone I respect this much is telling me to think about things differently, then I should take careful notice. He has clearly been out in the world and seen things far beyond this environment, this place of constantly keeping score and endless report cards and rushing from one competition to the next, and so he is someone I have always paid attention to. There are a few teachers like this – those who will take us to one side now and then, to offer advice and encouragement – and he is the one I value most.

Our exchange that day is only a short one, but it is one of the most important conversations of my life. The way he communicates with me, his firmness and his compassion and his call for greater empathy, will stay with me for ever. Who the hell am I, I think, to judge people I don't know? How dare I? I tell myself to do better. I don't want to go around hurting people. I don't want to disappoint him again. The gentle soul later becomes a dear friend of mine, and turns out to be heterosexual; years later, as it happens, I do not.

THE ANIMAL SOUNDS

If you are at any boarding school for long enough, you will either witness or execute just about every prank there is. On the morning of one school holiday, I walk down to one of the schoolyards to find that someone has covered a 150-year-old cannon from one of history's most famous sieges in neon paint. Another time, I walk down to one of the school fields to discover that someone – a team of boys, surely, there can't have been just one of them – has bleached the image of a vast penis and accompanying testes across its surface. And then there is my favourite prank: the animal sounds. Every few weeks my year has an assembly in the school theatre, and there is always a gap of a couple of minutes between the closing of the theatre doors and the arrival of the speaker at the lectern. That gap is when all the lights in the theatre go off, and when the students, as loud as they can, begin to bellow, wail, roar or howl almost every sound I might hear in the rainforest or jungle – I hear perfect impersonations of apes, tigers and parakeets. Once, just before the lights go down, I see one boy rise from his seat, his paws to his chest, his jaw yawning, about to become a cat of the night.

The prank is a tool of amusement but also of revenge. One summer my house puts on a play, and at the end of its run I and the other boys in my year, being the youngest in the house, have the task of putting all the props away. There is a fair bit to carry, and so I am not amused when one of the boys shirks his duties and scurries home to bed, his excuse being that he has classes early tomorrow.

I protest that we all have classes early tomorrow, but he is already gone.

While I, disgruntled, carry on with the work, one of my friends has a plan. He's not getting away with that, he says. Once I have tidied everything up, he walks over to one of the props, the head of a horse costume, and heads out of the theatre.

My friend gets back to the house about half an hour after the deserter, who helpfully lives on the bottom floor of my boarding house. The deserter, desperate for his beauty sleep, is already in bed and beginning to slumber, which makes him the perfect target. His bedroom window is wide open, to welcome in the balmy evening; and so, my friend dons the horse's head, puts his head in through the window, and then begins to nuzzle the sleeping boy. He slowly wakes to find a horse rubbing its face against his nose, and howls in horror as the accursed animal retreats gleefully through the curtains and disappears back into the void.

THE DISGUST LUNGING

In five years of being at school, I only catch the train home with my friends on one occasion. Almost all of them live in London, mostly to its west, and so they normally get the express train directly into one of the city's main terminals. Even though I live in a suburb closer to school than they do, they arrive home before me.

Today, though, they have chosen to take the train with me. Maybe that's because the weather is unusually good, and they are feeling leisurely as a result. Or perhaps they are just enjoying the conversation with me, which started as I walked over the bridge from school and into the neighbouring town, from where I caught the connecting train that brought me here. Maybe both, I don't know, but now I'm on the slow train towards London, and I am feeling anxious. Until now, no one from school has seen where I live, and I am worried about what they will think.

There are only four stops to my station, but my train comes only every half hour. That's fine, though – it gives me more time to prepare for the moment when I finally disembark. I am therefore distracted as my friends talk about what they will be doing for their holidays, only vaguely hearing what they are saying. Some of them will be staying overnight at each other's houses, which to me is almost unimaginable. I was raised never to overstay my welcome in someone's home, taught to remember that families are furiously private places where after a certain and very short time a friendly newcomer becomes an intruder. Some of them are even going abroad, to a second or third family home.

My train rolls through the outskirts of London, which to my relief are pleasingly green today – I don't want my friends to think my surroundings are dreary and industrial. But as I approach West Drayton, my stop, I feel a sharply rising anxiety, and then my high street comes into view, a shabby collection of local stores and office blocks.

Oh my God, says one of my classmates, the disgust lunging from his throat. I mumble a goodbye as I turn and head out through the creaking door of the carriage, the shame rolling down over my shoulders like a cloak.

I TOOK FLIGHT

They sense me entering the field at once.

It is a summer afternoon, one of those days so far into the holidays that I have forgotten the actual day of the week, and I have taken my BMX bike for a ride alongside the river that connects my town to the next one. To track the river a little better, I cycle off the pavement next to the main road and through a gap someone has torn in the green wire fence, the high grass rustling against the spokes of my wheels. After a few minutes the river thins to a stream, crossed by a narrow bridge. I head across the bridge slowly – there are no railings – and through a gang of trees, clustered shoulder to shoulder like onlookers at the edge of a crash scene. As I pass through the trees, I find myself in a field, but before my back wheel is even out of the woods, they already know I am there.

A hundred and fifty metres away, a group of around a dozen white teenagers are sunbathing in a circle in the centre of the field: most of them are boys; most of the boys are topless; all of them are wearing sports kit – tracksuit bottoms and white trainers. They all turn to face me as I move in their direction, somehow detecting my arrival, white blood cells alerted by an intruder. Suddenly the field is an artery and I am the foreign threat, and two of the blood cells are dispatched to meet me, leaping onto the back of nearby motorbikes and riding round in a wide loop, gathering speed as they approach me. I knew at once that they would hunt me and so I have already turned, surging back out through the trees and soaring over the bridge, the glint of my retreating spokes glistening over the water. I cut across the main road and down a quiet street, then double back on myself to make sure the motorbikes are no longer in pursuit; but they must have stopped long ago, their riders probably amused at the haste with which I took flight.

IF THE REVEREND HAD STAYED

There is something so safe about this school. Even when I encounter difficulty here, there is an underlying sense of protection, that everything will be okay. There is always a figure of authority close by, and there are even a few boys who have their own security details. At times that atmosphere creates a tremendous warmth, a true camaraderie. I remember the time when some students from prominent families arrived at my school and the whole community embraced them in the gentlest way, gave them the room to be themselves, and they ended up thriving. I will never be prouder of my school than in that period, of how everyone pulled together.

There are many days, when work is going well and I am getting on with everyone in my house, where it is idyllic here. I stroll out onto the lawn in summer for the house photo, the grass ruffling my ankles, and I wander along the riverbank, listening to the happy splash of the water against the oars. I go out onto the main sports fields and play five-a-side football for hours, bringing out my stereo so that I can accompany my games with a soundtrack, forming bonds with friends and acquaintances that will last a lifetime. There are even entire terms where I look back and think, yes, that was a job well done. There is a great certainty about those days – the knowledge that if I put in an exceptional effort in the classroom, I will receive abundant rewards. This, of course, is perfect training for life in the corporate world.

This is why so many people who grow up in environments of such comfort can be so unsympathetic to those who don't. They simply have no concept of a society where, even if people work their very hardest, everything can still fall apart for the majority of them. They have been raised in a realm where every personal downfall is self-inflicted – a wealthy kid caught with drugs, or with a girl in his room after hours, or slacking in exams. The idea that you can simply be overwhelmed by your circumstances is utterly alien to them. This is not a system that fails them, and so they not only learn to trust it but to treat it as the norm. It quickly becomes the prism through which they see everything.

Each term I go home from this to my quietly crumbling suburb, with its local parks, which at one point didn't receive a single pound sterling in investment for years, not even a new coat of paint on the climbing frames or a replacement for the broken gates or cracked swings, and it is this contrast that just about allows me to retain a grasp on reality. I never quite forget that there are people who do not get the support from their surroundings that they deserve. The core of my community is the Methodist church, where the reverend makes a point of inviting everyone to lunch with his family, even the ones who, some of the congregation mutter, are a little too troubled, even the one who put his brother in the tumble dryer with a view to turning it on but thankfully didn't. That reverend acts as a mentor and a surrogate uncle, and he is so beloved that when he moves away to the countryside, my church hires a minibus and drives a couple of hours out there to surprise him. When he sees our vehicle turn into the yard, his face is a sunrise of joy. I will never forget him and his family standing in the fading light to wave us away the last time I see him, the heart of my village, who had to move away.

I wonder how much better my town would have been if the reverend had stayed; it was so much less warm after his departure. The great thing about my school, unlike my home town, is that it can keep its best people. The finest teachers rarely move on for superior job opportunities because there aren't many out there better than this. I have friends who drop in on their tutors for years after they have left, and who have become ever closer to them as time passes. My school gets to hang on to its reverends, and it is all the richer for it.

NOT GETTING MY SUPERBODY

I don't do much in my summer holidays other than the odd job, either packing solvents at the local factory or sorting documents at a nearby warehouse; the rest of the time I work on my writing, which is what I truly wish to do with my life. Encouraged by my success in a poetry competition and then a short-story contest, I work on several novels, but none of them come anywhere close to being published. This is partly because I am still young and learning my craft, but also because my writing style is far too frantic: I am trying to do too much with each sentence. I am trying to make every phrase spectacular.

Perhaps the most positive thing that happens in my home town during my teens is that the council builds a basketball court in the park near my house, which means that the local kids finally have a place to hang around that isn't a bus stop. During my holidays I go down there whenever possible, and I slowly improve my game, helped by the visit of my cousins from North America one summer. They are vastly better than me, taking one step and one second to make a decision whenever I take two, but by the time they leave I am so much faster than before, and they have spent so long slapping the ball back into my face that eventually I have learned how to shoot. One day I even manage to dunk before they have a chance to pay attention, and they are furious because they suspect I will never shut up about it, and they are correct.

The first time I dunk I think, My God, that is one of the ten things I had to do or see before I could die happy. This is one of the things that I feel black boys should be able to do and it is a consolation for not getting my superbody. You know the superbody – the one that all black men seem to develop as soon as they breach the borders of puberty, at which point the muscles burst forth from their shirts and they reach steepling heights; the type that attracts the local girls, and that intimidates racists into silence.

I couldn't wait to become one of those black men, the ones I have so often seen on television, who seem to have been given these extraordinary physiques as a form of armour against the world. But my superbody will never arrive.

I don't know anything about dating girls, so I listen to both my older cousins and the other boys in the neighbourhood who do. One of them says that I will never feel so much like a man as when a girl is on her knees giving me oral sex. The boy says it with a sneer on his face, *on her knees*. The other boys and I are at that age where, when we are talking to each other, we don't actually wait for anyone to finish their sentences but leap in whenever we see a pause so that we can tell the next and funnier joke. In some cases, we will always be that age.

A CULTURAL THING

Over the course of two or three summers during my mid-teens, my home town changes so much. For a long time, my family was one of the few black families in my area, and suddenly there are several more of us. We try to work out where they have come from, and I conclude that most of them have moved out from the centre of the capital to its outskirts, forced there by rising property prices.

We don't get to know them so well, mainly because their children are a little younger than us, but we find it unusual suddenly to be part of a growing demographic. I am long accustomed to being the only black person in most rooms that I enter. If I want to see large numbers of those who look like me, I will typically have to travel into the city. Out here, my family has a quiet, dutiful presence, carefully leaving little trace.

My own street is a good example of my invisibility. Despite sharing my road with eleven other homes, I will only get to know a handful of their occupants in the two decades I live there. The neighbour to whom I am closest, a boy a few years older than me who lives in the house on my left, will die of cancer in his teens. I won't remember a word he said to me, but I will always remember his friendship, his gentleness. His kindness reminds me of the first of my mother's friends that I recall meeting, that time we drove hundreds of miles north to endure an even colder winter. My mother's friend, a dark-haired woman whose mouth seemed to smile even when it was at rest, took me through shin-deep snow, her laughter dancing through the air as I went.

Over the years, I wonder why my neighbours aren't more open, more welcoming. Maybe, I think, it is a cultural thing. For a few years a family moves into the largest house in the corner of the street, and life in my cul-de-sac is immediately more exciting. They are from the other side of the world and they introduce themselves at once, their happiness and exuberance almost bewildering. They have a dog who is so enthusiastic when he sees me that, at first, I think he is trying to eat me. They hold regular barbecues to which they invite everyone nearby, and whenever the mother talks her voice is about a third louder than everyone else's. I love them immediately.

They move out and I don't see them again, but they were a taste of what was coming. As time goes on my town becomes louder. Years later, when I am almost forty, I will return to my home town around Christmas and visit the local supermarket to pick up the last few items for dinner, and I will notice something striking: as I walk through aisle after aisle, I see very few white faces; the customers there now have heritages from all over the world. I see this as a gift, but I also have the same uneasy feeling that I had one winter when I taught a classroom of students from the city, and I looked at the surnames to see that every single one was visibly foreign in origin. Oh no, I thought then, some people are not going to like this.

SO OVERWHELMED THAT HE CANNOT WEEP

My cousins are in town for the funeral of my grandfather. He dies at the age of seventy-eight, and my mother tells me later that I was the last person to pass him something to eat or drink. He has passed away due to his second stroke, which they say is generally fatal. His first stroke came when he heard the news of my father's death. The last phrase he spoke before he collapsed, delivered in his own language and in a speech that he gave to members of the community, was, *We shall overcome, we shall overcome, we shall overcome.*

My relatives come from all over the world, and I stop counting after the fortieth one of them arrives. One night we jump in a convoy of cars just after midnight and drive down to the centre of the city, playing music with eerie and thrilling basslines all the way down the motorway, the vocals so deep they thud against my breastplate. Who is this? I ask in wonder, and one of my cousins says, That's Wu-Tang.

Several listens of Wu-Tang later, the day of my grandfather's funeral arrives. His body is on display in an open coffin and many dozens, perhaps hundreds, of people file past to pay their respects. My cousins and I are all wearing traditional dress, these beautiful cotton shirts as long and wide as American football jerseys, stitched from red, yellow, black and golden thread. The air in the small church is humid with grief; I turn to look at one of my relatives and he is so overwhelmed that he cannot weep.

That evening I go for dinner at the house where my grandparents lived together, where they spent the last of their fifty-three years of marriage. After I eat, I walk down the corridor towards the living room, where my grandmother is standing in the middle of the rug. She is trembling, and when I am still a few yards from the doorway I hear her begin to howl, the sound you can only make when you have lost someone who has held your hand and walked with you to the very corners of your soul and told you, It is okay, thank you so much for inviting me, it is wonderful in here, and she falls towards her knees and most of my aunts surround her, catching her, protecting her, and then one of them sees me watching and slams the door. It is the only time I will see my grandmother cry.

A DAMAGING NARRATIVE

I walk into the school theatre with all the other boys in my year, ready to learn where I have finished in my year's end-of-term examinations. On the previous two occasions my results have placed me in the top thirty-two out of 255 students, which means that if I finish within that group again, I will earn a scholarship. I sit in the middle of a row about halfway up the hall. One of my tutors begins to count down the list of surnames, starting with the student who finished in 128th place. I am confident that I have not come that low, so I listen out carefully for my name to be mentioned. The numbers keep descending, in batches of four and five. Though the surnames are being read at an even pace it seems that my tutor's voice is speeding up. Fifty. I still haven't heard my name. Forty. My God, I have done it. I have done it!

I hear my name in thirty-fourth place.

The tears are out of my eyes before I even feel them rising. I convulse in my seat, my entire body rocking with sobs. I barely hear anyone else's name after that. All I can think about is the failure, my God, the failure. All this hard work, everything I was building with furious and painstaking care, shattered in an instant. My mother has made so many sacrifices for me to be here and all I had to do was work hard and do well in class and I couldn't even do that. I crush my face into my palms and by the time I raise my swollen eyes to look at the room around me the theatre is deserted.

No one mocks me for my heartbroken reaction to this result. Maybe that's because they are generally kind people, or because they were in that room with me too and they know the kind of pressure that being so regularly and publicly tested can generate. When I get home, I can barely discuss this devastating outcome with my mother. I slowly begin to look at myself as someone who can never quite deliver when it matters, who isn't quite gifted enough to get that lucky break, for whom the only way to succeed is sheer, undeniable brilliance, who has to create work that is not only accomplished but original, for whom merely working their hardest is not good enough. It is a damaging narrative with which I will attack myself whenever possible.

SHE REMINDS HIM OF HIS MAID

I will never forget the day I am talking to someone who is very friendly with one of the wealthiest people in the school. One day, when describing his friend – someone who regards him as his closest confidant – he tells me that the best thing about him is that at the end of the day he is fucking rich.

I think about the fucking rich boy, and at some level I actually find myself feeling sorry for him. How must it feel to have even your best friend describe you like that? But then I think to myself: the fucking rich boy already knows how he is perceived. He is too shrewd, too self-aware. Whenever I see him surrounded by people, he always seems slightly detached, as if he is just passing through. I know that detachment because I share it with him. Years later, I encounter his confidant, and, unsurprisingly, it sounds as though he and the fucking rich boy are not in contact any more.

I talk to another boy in the school, someone whose family has unimaginable wealth. He tells me that his father told him one thing in particular: to never forget that people always know exactly who you are and where you are from. Though wealthy people are not inherently different from the rest of the world, they are generally raised with a very different mentality. There is a watchfulness about many of them, a constant vigilance. Some of them keep their wealth as private as some might keep their faith.

It is often said that the more money some people have, the scruffier they are, and in some cases that is true. I see boys whose families have billions in assets wearing clothing that could disintegrate at any moment. Their favourite garments seem to be those drooping woollen sweaters that are apparently attacked nightly by a platoon of moths. But there are the others, the ones about whom I'd never guess. In my late twenties I go to dinner with an old schoolfriend, and in the course of the conversation he reveals that he is not from a middle-class family as most people thought, but from one of the biggest corporate dynasties in the country of his birth. I burst out laughing at that, incredulous that he could have kept such a thing so quiet. Those who knew, knew, he shrugged, and smiled. What I realise over time is that, even at a school like mine, there are elites within elites; that wealth is a secret language, its rules elusive and its speakers even more so. My schoolfriend never once acted as if he were superior to others, never wore anything that looked remotely expensive; but, then again, he chose a career as far as possible from his upbringing at the earliest opportunity, probably showing that he never truly defined himself by his origins, much as they might try to define him.

There are other friends I grew up with whose wealth I knew about from the early days, and, if anything, I over-compensated for that gap in our resources. I will never forget the time when, as a university student, I went for a meal with one of them. At the end of our lunch the bill came, and before he had a chance to get any money out I had already paid the bulk of it. He will meet my mother once. Later, smiling fondly, he will tell me that she reminds him of his maid.

A BRIEF ILLNESS

For a certain period in my teens, the reminder of death arrives at my house every two weeks. There, on top of the piano and propped up next to a pot of flowers, is a small white card inviting me to a funeral. The funeral is always that of a refugee from Northern Uganda, my family's part of the country, and they have typically passed away in their late twenties or early thirties after a brief illness. The funeral always takes place somewhere in the furthest reaches of south London, in an area that seems far too leafy to be truly part of the city. On that Sunday I will put on my only suit, a shade of light grey that only children up to a certain age seem to wear, and dutifully stuff myself into the back of an overcrowded car.

When I arrive at the funeral, I will meet countless men and women with superbly polished skin even darker than my own, each of whom will tell me that they held me as a child. The ceremony will sometimes take place in a church but more often in a community centre that has been hired for the occasion. I understand little of what is said in the service, but the sheer depth of everyone's grief means I don't need to. After the service, I and the other children stand in one corner of the courtyard with plates of chicken and rice while the adults discuss politics. Though they are far out of earshot, I know they are discussing politics because I have not been invited to join them. I will stand there until my legs ache and then become so numb that they stop aching, and then it will be time to go home.

I do not go to every one of the funerals, but someone from my family always seems to do so, to pay their respects. No one ever talks about the brief illness, though we all know what it is. No one will ever say the word

AIDS: it is as if it is too shameful to be uttered. It is as if AIDS is the cruel aftershock of two decades that have seen my ethnic group, the Acholi, sustain horrifying losses at the hands of two successive despots. There are constant rumours that several of the Acholi were imprisoned by their opponents and injected with this illness before they left Uganda, thus catalysing the spread of a virus that had already proven to be devastating. Maybe, I muse, that is just what war does: some victims it murders straight away, and with the others, the initially grateful survivors, it takes its slow and sadistic time.

The rumours about the injections continue long after the series of funerals comes to an end. It is always rumour – the war, even though it is now hundreds of months and thousands of miles away, is still discussed in low voices and behind closed doors, as if it were a violently jealous lover. Years later, when I am working as a journalist, I will meet a fellow member of our ethnic group in east London, and he will ask me why I am not doing more to help my people back home. Look at my surname, I tell him, it is on every byline that I write; there is no hiding who I am or where I am from, and I don't want to hide it either. Look at all the political topics I write about. Just because you do not see me around, it does not mean that I do not care. I am angrier at him than I thought I would be. How much more do you want us to give? I will think bitterly. We already gave you my dad.

THE FEAR OF BEING OUTNUMBERED

There will be a time in future when I will think that the nation is in trouble, and when that day comes, I will always think back to a conversation I had with a taxi driver in my mid-twenties, a few years after leaving school. During a friendly enough chat, the subject comes round to how my family came to the country, and I proudly tell him the story of how my mother escaped a war with nothing more than the possessions in her hand luggage, and then made her way as a doctor. The driver listens reasonably; he feels that he can talk openly with me. He feels that the immigrants are changing his way of life too much. I know that he is not making a personal attack on me – he really seems to like me – it is just obvious that he is feeling overwhelmed, and he wants things back to how they were. I ponder what he might mean by how things were, and I understand that he probably means life as it was in my cul-de-sac, when there weren't too many of us to make a significant visual difference to mostly white community life. I understand that he has a fear I have never had, the fear of being outnumbered, and that there is nothing I can do to make him feel comfortable about that.

I will hear or see many versions of the same remarks over the coming years, how some white people will walk down a high street or a train carriage and feel like outsiders in their own country. It is a feeling that shows me that many of them are much more self-aware about racism than they often admit – that they are conscious of the challenges of being on the fringes, that they would not want any part of that for themselves. From my experience, I know that being a minority is fine so long as the majority thinks well of me, but I also know that such favour has historically been hard to achieve.

THE MASK

I will never forget the look he gives me. It must have taken centuries of wealth and resentment to perfect that glare. His eyes carry no ordinary contempt: goodness knows how many parental rants and angry dinner-table conversations about lower souls like me have been poured into the two bitter little crystals of hate that now glisten out at me. I have played reasonably aggressive sport and I have been in a handful of fights, but I will recall nothing so violent from those encounters as the feeling he has just conveyed without even touching me.

The way he delivers the look is almost artful. He looks over his shoulder at me, first down towards one of my ankles, then raising his head slowly upwards, as if his gaze is scanning my body for some socially undesirable barcode. By the time his eyes briefly meet mine I have long ago run out of smart things to say. It is a mercy when he does not attempt conversation, because his fury looks non-negotiable. For the next three years, I am stuck in this place with him. I will have to endure him in the queue for school assemblies and encounter him in the same narrow lanes.

It is because of encounters like this that I learn the mask: to hide my true feelings unless it is absolutely necessary, placing those emotions beneath a heavy clothing of civility. What else am I supposed to do? I can't exactly walk around falling out with people – this is a boarding school, not a day school where I can escape my adversaries. If I make enemies that afternoon, I'll see them in the dinner queue that evening. I'll run into them that weekend in the library or the chapel. It's just not worth it.

I first learned the mask at my prep school, where I started off by trying to settle every confrontation there and then – Where I come from, I will assert at first, people always say things to my face – but then I quickly understood that this was not how combat was handled in this new environment. This was not a world of fights but of feuds. Rage was rarely expressed there and then. Instead it simmered, becoming bitterness.

Long after I leave school, I will find that the mask is hard to shift. Years later, one partner of mine will say that she is never quite sure what I am thinking. Another one will say that even when I am at my most intimate, I am still not fully there. Perhaps I think I still need it. Perhaps I always will.

THE LOVING HATE

I will forever regret not taking a photo of that car-park wall.

I am in my mid-teens. The car park is directly next to the supermarket, which is to its right, just behind the local basketball court and beside the church. It has room for perhaps a couple of hundred vehicles, but with the exception of Saturdays it is rarely that busy. Cutting through the car park is the quickest way to get to the main road, and so I walk through here at least twice a week. I enter it by coming down a long avenue, then taking a right, then a left; I stride between two high fences on either side, towards that vast car-park wall, some eighty metres across, then under a large archway and on towards the main road.

One day I am sauntering across the tarmac when I see something on that vast wall that wasn't there a couple of days ago. A blanket of brash Technicolor paint, it looks like a mural, but as I move closer I see that it is instead a mosaic of images of various sizes, which appear to have been stencilled there. I don't recognise all of the symbols, but the ones I do are more than enough. British National Party. National Front. Ku Klux Klan.

After my initial shock I step nearer and think about the rank of racial hatred, and about how this is now truly dangerous. When it comes to racism, I have come to understand that there is a pyramid of danger. The British National Party are at the bottom corners. If I encounter one of the BNP, they are merely angry, more likely to rant at me than anything else. Maybe a threat of physical violence, but nothing too much worse than that. The National Front – the NF – they are something else; they are higher up that pyramid. Maybe halfway. I fully expect them to deliver upon a promise of harm. I have not yet seen one of them, but I imagine them to be no different from a gang of weapon-wielding Nazis. Then there is Combat 18, which I have just discovered. And then there is the KKK, and everyone knows about them. They are at the very tip, and thankfully we don't really see them in the UK. They are the type to drag us from our houses and lynch us in our own gardens. Decades later, theirs is the stencilled symbol I will remember best: the three Ks, one of them stacked upon the other, in the middle of a bright-red star.

What are the KKK doing here? I think numbly. They are American. And then it comes to me: that last night, or whenever this collage of cruelty was made, someone stood just where I stood, their body filled with a calm, steady, patient hate, the loving hate, the kind of hate that paints itself across walls with gentle and intricate detail, the hand that dutifully lowers the lever of the gas chamber. What a set of footsteps to walk in. Shortly afterwards it is cleaned away, but I will never forget it.

BE STRONG, OR BE QUICK

A few months after I see this carefully crafted graffiti, I see posters in my home town announcing that the anti-fascists will soon be marching there, so I check the dates carefully to make sure that I am not out on the streets then. I worry that these activists will make the problem worse, that by bringing their protest to my suburb they will further escalate the fury that I have felt simmering against black people. What happens the evening after, when they have finished striding down my roads, brandishing their bright banners? What backlash will they create once they have gone?

It hasn't occurred to me yet that the presence of anti-racists near where I live will actually discourage those who despise me. If I am honest with myself, I am afraid of seeing the hate up close. I am still not used to looking into the eyes of someone who views me as a target, who might one day work out where I live. I am still too fearful of confrontation for that; the first time that I march against the far right will be a quarter of a century later, in another country.

In my teens, I have worked out a very easy method of dealing with racism in the street: be strong, or be quick. I am not strong, but I can hold a good, sustained sprint. If it ever comes to the point that someone confronts me in the street, all I need is two feet of space to get past them, and then I will be gone. I am confident of that; and since I am quick, since I can flee, I see no reason why I should stand my ground.

AND SO JOHN IT WAS

One day I decide to call myself something else. As a black boy from a strict household, I am well aware of the opportunity that my education has given me, and I am terrified of messing up that chance. I see how black boys get in trouble with police, who every now and then seem to stop people who look like me for fun. I also notice how, if I was to hang around with the other kids in the area a fair bit, they might add my name to their graffiti across town, spraying it loud, high and wide across the walls of the basketball court, the car park, the bus stops and everywhere else they could find. To them, tagging my name alongside theirs on public property would be a compliment, a sign that I was someone of note in the town, but to me it would help to make me a target. I have a very distinctive name, and I don't want it to end up on that graffiti in case the police start seeing it and think, Ah, so this is another person we should be looking out for. I don't want to be on people's radar like that. And so, from about the age of thirteen, I start telling people in my area that my name is John.

It is surprisingly simple to get away with this lie since I don't know all that many people in my home town. For one thing, I don't have much of a social life during my holidays. Since my mother is wary of the local area, I don't get to go out in the evenings till I am in my late teens. During that time, too, I am not in touch with anyone from school; it won't be until I am seventeen years old that I pick up the phone and call a friend. My two lives, at home and at school, are wholly separate, primed for disguise.

And so John it was: simple, English, generic. The only

time I regularly see anyone from the local area is at the basketball court, or on the way to and from the shops, and so the deceit is easy. I don't remember the first day I decided to do it, or when I started answering to it. What I do remember is the first time I saw someone scribble graffiti in tribute to my fake name on the wooden fence surrounding the basketball court; and then feeling a quiet pride that my subterfuge had worked, that I had avoided detection.

HE WAS NICKNAMED SUPERMAN

I don't really have any close friends in my home town. The ones who come nearest to fitting that description are two boys with whom I play basketball whenever I am back from school for my half-term or end-of-term holidays. One of them has parents from Iraq, the other from Nigeria. Despite hanging out for years, we don't really know any detail about each other's lives. I will never know how many, if any, siblings they might have, what their parents do for a living, and somehow it doesn't matter. There is such a simplicity and an innocence to our friendship.

In the space of a couple of summers, the three of us will

get good enough at basketball that as a team we can beat pretty much anyone who comes down to our local court. There is a mostly friendly rivalry with a group of men in their mid-twenties from the neighbouring town; they turn up most midweek evenings in sports cars and jeans uncomfortably stuffed with muscle. The only time things get tense is when one of them has an argument with one of my cousins. I take my cousin's side, and afterwards my opponent tells me, You don't do that; you should never do that; you should always side with someone from your area.

Not many girls come down to the court. The ones who do are about my age and tend to be pursued by the men who are ten years older. One of the guys who stands out the most is a nineteen-year-old who always wears the same outfit: a black baseball cap – backwards – with dark blue jeans, a tight black T-shirt and a silver chain. He never plays basketball with us, but he leans on the fence at the corner of the court as if it is his prop. He has a detached air, which I interpret not as shyness but confidence. He rarely looks happy, which is as I expect: the one thing I do know about sex is that the boys in my area who sleep with the most girls tend not to smile very much.

One of my closer friends is dating someone his own age, who he meets when he is about fifteen and who I will see him with each time I return to town long after I have moved away. She is always kind and excited to hear what I've been up to on my travels, and at first it surprises me that people as worldly as them are so happy living within the confines of these same few streets. After a while, though, I begin to understand her attachment to this suburb.

One of the other men I see regularly at the court is said to have spent a few years in a Russian prison, where he calmly endured so many beatings from the officers that he was nicknamed Superman. I never ask him if this is true, but I never doubt it: I cannot imagine anyone who could beat this man unless there were a pack of them. He seems to live out of a van, in which he takes off across mainland Europe for a few months at a time. The last time I see him, he has just come back from Germany; I have been away at school, and to my disbelief he greets me warmly. Seeing him laugh is as shocking as watching a shark playing fetch. Emboldened by his happiness to see me, I finally ask why it is that he keeps coming back to here of all places when he has the world to choose from. John, he says, there's no place like home.

THE LEAST BRITISH OF THINGS

One day I am with a younger relative and I board the bus to go to the neighbouring town. The bus driver looks at us both, and then asks that I pay the full fare for my relative. She's only twelve, I protest, but the driver insists. Bemused, a little irritated, I pay the full fare for both of us and take my seat. After a couple of minutes, my relative leans over to me and says, I think the bus driver is racist.

What do you mean? I say, and she says, Look at how angry he was when he asked you for the money. It was the way he looked at me and then spoke to you. Maybe he did think you were old enough to pay the adult fare, I suggest, but she shakes her head; she says she doesn't think it was that. I keep an eye on who gets onto the bus for the next few stops, and to my disbelief and then my anger I see tall two white girls who don't look a day under fifteen getting onto the bus, paying child fares, then giving oblivious smiles as they walk past us to the back.

My fury takes me to the front of the bus to do the least British of things, which is to talk to the driver while the vehicle is still in motion. It has always been in me to speak up, and the first time I remember doing so was in Uganda, a few days after my dad's funeral. I was four years old and in my family's house in Kampala when my dad's own sister turned up with a lorry full of armed soldiers and proceeded to rob us of all the valuable possessions that they could find before our helpless eyes. She had always been resentful of his money, and she correctly assumed that this was the perfect time to loot. As the soldiers loaded the last of our things into the lorry, I – being too young and stupid to know better – ran down to the front of the house and slapped my aunt on the hip. She turned, and I can still remember her laughing down at me, her face framed by the sun.

Excuse me, I tell the driver, we have a problem. I stand next to his booth while I wait for the bus to stop for the next passenger and then I continue. You charged us for two full fares, but you made those last two girls pay child fares, even though they are clearly over the age for that.

He looks up at me, his eyes two dark brown pools of contempt. We have a problem, I tell him, before he can speak. The problem begins with the letter R and we both know what it is but neither of us is going to say it. He opens his mouth in outrage and I think, I've got you.

As he yells, I grow calmer, listening as he protests that people like me always bring up things like that, always play that card, and at one point his syllables flow together in a sort of wordless moan, as if he were speaking to me underwater. I will take your driver's number, I inform him, speaking slowly and gently, and I will make a complaint. Go on then, he says, and I make a great show of noting down the digits, even though I know at once that I won't do anything with them, that I don't trust his boss to be bothered. My stop arrives shortly, just at the edge of the small roundabout that leads to the shopping centre, and I let my relative off first before I disembark. Instead of walking into the mall, I wait there because I know that the bus needs to come past me on its way out of the street. As it rolls towards me, I make eye contact with the driver. He jerks his clenched fist at me, but he is trapped in there, seething away as he sails by, and, smiling widely at him, I bow.

A SLAVE DRIVER

There is an incident of racism that occurs at school, which I cannot ascribe to mere ignorance and which I will never truly forgive or forget because I cannot believe that someone so focused in their hatred has actually changed. I don't hear the insult, but I am told about it, months later, maybe because the close and trusted friend who told me feared that my reaction would be volcanic, and maybe they were right.

I get into an argument with a boy and the exchange is a spirited one. He has been told I have been disrespecting his family, which I find strange because I do not even know who his family is or what they do. I tell him this and that I have no idea where the accusation came from, but despite my protests he does not believe me. A little later, as a class is just about to begin, he is overheard by a close friend saying that he hates me so much that he wishes he could tell me that his great-grandfather was a slave driver.

My friend tells me, and once I have absorbed this news I go and do some research, the irony being that I am finally in a position to talk about what the boy's family does for a living. My research reveals that the profession of the boy's great-grandfather very likely did involve the ownership of black people. From that day, my hatred for him will remain unashamed, unrelenting and total. In his final year at school, he ends up in a position of significant authority. It is interesting to me that, despite his stance on this issue, he has always been far from an outcast.

OTHER BLACK BOYS

Whenever I play sport against other private schools, I look out for the other black boys. I do this out of a form of solidarity, because I know how difficult it can be in a place where I always stand out, where I fear if I make a mistake, then news of it will travel further. I also know that several of those boys will either be from middle-class or working-class backgrounds, and so this world will be wholly alien to them, as it initially was to me. There's almost always a firm nod before a game and an especially firm handshake after it, a brief but complex gesture that says, *It's okay, my brother, I get it, you're doing great.*

It is sobering on the rare occasions when my salutes go unacknowledged. I greet one boy before a match and he looks at me, confused. I score three and a half goals a game, he warns me. He is a pretty good player and that day he scores two and a half fewer goals than usual. I wonder why he is dismissive of me and then I think that maybe, given that he goes to school in east London and does not board, seeing a black boy when he is out and about is as unremarkable as bumping into a fellow apple at the orchard.

There's another time, the one that hurts most, when a football match ends in a well-contested draw and I go over to the black guy on the other team to thank him for a fine game. As I approach, he is standing at the middle of a semicircle of his friends, all of whom are white, and I nod, and he nods back at me and then I extend my hand for him to shake it. He puts his hand out too and then, at the very last minute, he pulls it back and runs it through his hair, leaving my acknowledgement hovering there, my fingers clutching at air. He and his friends burst out laughing, then they all turn and walk off.

Humiliation sears through me for a moment and then I realise, Wait, he is probably their cool guy. Maybe that is just what he does: he performs for them. Perhaps he is at house parties with them and even though he does not rap, someone always ends up passing him the micro-phone; when hip-hop comes on at one of those parties, maybe there is an expectant pause as they wait for him to begin to dance. If that is the case, then good luck to him, because that is a pressure all of its own.

Luckily that experience is not the norm for me. My most affirming moment comes when I am playing basket-ball against a boarding school about a ninety-minute drive from mine; the school is a mixed one, so there are actual girls in the dining hall as we arrive for lunch, and I take great care to walk across the room with as casual a swagger as possible. I am so focused on appearing unfussed that I don't know if anyone actually sees me.

I head over to the gym with my teammates, and to my quiet excitement it looks as though some of the actual girls will be watching us play. The game is exhilarating. We are not expected to win, particularly not away from home and against opposition of this quality, but our point guard is sublime that day, his jump shot as elegant as a sunbeam. He scores about half our team's points, I add thirteen, and we triumph by sixty-one points to fifty-three. Yet the game's outstanding player, narrowly ahead of my point guard, is a black guy on the opposing team, whose moves are so skilful that I nod in approval after a couple of his baskets.

At the final buzzer, I jog over to him and we embrace. We talk and it turns out he is off to study engineering at univer-sity; he clearly can't wait to get out there and do it, and I am thrilled for him. Keep up the great work, I tell him. You too, brother, he replies, and we part. Yes, I think, this is why I am doing it; this matters, and meeting other black boys like him makes my own lonely journey that little bit easier; we are two drivers on an otherwise deserted motorway, flashing our headlights as we pass each other in the dusk.

HE CARES TOO MUCH

There is one schoolboy I know who is obsessed with politics like most boys my age are obsessed with football, and I think it strange that someone should be so interested in power so young. I have already come to think of politics as dangerous. Whenever my family discusses current affairs in the country of my heritage, the routine is the same: my grandfather sits in the furthest corner of his living room, and his children, including my mother, sit in a semicircle around him; there is then a pause as I, my siblings and cousins are ushered out, and then the adults talk until the early hours of the morning. We all sit in the kitchen or on the staircase, bored but with no choice other than to wait until our parents are ready to give us a lift home. None of us ever so much as eavesdrop at the living-room door; we have too much respect for what is going on behind it.

When my grandparents arrive in the country, it is never fully explained what they have run from; each year I get more of the picture – a death of a relative here, a disappearance of a friend there. At first I am frustrated, and then I realise that they are merely making an effort to protect me. They would tell me more, but they are worried I will get too emotional. Take the example of my great-uncle. He was due to be executed, and the night before he was set to face the firing squad he escaped his hotel, where he was just about to have the last supper of his life with his executioner, and fled over the border disguised as an imam. My family don't want me to know those stories yet and I won't hear this one until I am in my early thirties. They don't want to fill my head with politics; they want me to study.

That is why when I see my peer at school talking about politics with the joy that I talk about sport, I am a little unsettled. These are people's lives, I think. The boy rants about several things that make people roll their eyes, but I always listen carefully. He hates the European Union with a startling passion at a time when I am barely aware what the European Union is. That boy, I think, is too intense about these things, he cares too much. Maybe his family always ask him to join all those conversations about politics that I am not yet invited to. Later, at university, I will see him standing outside the student union building, complaining loudly about the same subject. No one is paying much attention to him. I go over to him and swiftly realise how much pleasure he takes from irritating whoever stops to listen, so I get on with my day.

At first it is striking, given how many Etonians go on to become politicians, how few of them talk about it as a future career. But then it makes sense: like most other teenagers, it is simply too soon to get that serious. All of that can wait until university at the very least, or until you get out into the world and decide which positions of authority appeal to you the most.

One of the few political issues that many boys seem most passionate about is fox hunting. They are worried people will try to ban it, but they are the only people who seem to talk about it. I suspect if they just stopped talking about fox hunting – a hobby that, under even casual examination, many would find abhorrent – and quietly got on with it, then no one would bother them. But I also suspect this is about something more: it is to boast proudly of a hobby that others would reject.

THE HATE IN TIME

The man's eyes only meet mine for the briefest time, but they have already shown me enough. I am walking to visit the optician with my sister one summer afternoon when the man passes me; he is coming from underneath the railway bridge, near the pub with the chalk marks on its walls, and all the way through my appointment I won't be able to stop thinking about his stare. It is as startling as scalding water.

He is slightly taller than me, thin, lean, his hair a short brown furrow, his hands plunged into the pockets of his black leather bomber jacket. He is walking at a purposeful pace but the moment he sees me he begins to slow slightly; I have made him curious, and as I walk past him and under the bridge, I don't have to look back to know that he has stopped. My sister has not noticed any of this.

I come out of the appointment about forty minutes later. The optician's office is not far from the railway bridge, maybe twenty metres or so, but the shadow under the bridge is so dense that I can't see all the way through to the other side. I have a feeling that the man is still there.

Let's cross the road here, I tell my sister, and seeing the concern on my face she follows me without asking why. I walk through the train station and out into the yard, where I wait for the double-decker bus, and it is only when I climb to the top floor and sit at the very front that I start to relax. The bus pulls out of the yard and begins to turn right, up the hill and away from the railway bridge, and I lean forward, looking for the man.

He is still there, standing a few yards from where I passed him about an hour ago. He has been waiting for me, in the hope that I would return the way I came. He looks up as the bus approaches and his eyes meet mine again, but this time there is not hate, there is almost warmth.

He smiles at me and shakes his head a little – Well played – and then he unzips his jacket, hooking his thumbs into its folds so that he can pull it apart and show me what is in there.

His jacket is lined with a patchwork of colourful cotton squares, and each of them displays a swastika. They are various different colours and sizes: red, white and black; yellow, black and purple. The man grins up at me: Good work, you got me this time. The bus rolls up the hill and away, but that image will always stay with me, along with the thought of what might have happened if I hadn't spotted the hate in time.

I AM WU-TANG DARK

One day, on the way to a football match, a teammate asks me what I am listening to, and I tell him it's the latest release by the Wu-Tang Clan. He asks sharply why I would listen to that, and I don't like his tone, so I tell him, with equal disdain, Because it's my culture. He bursts out laughing, and I feel suitably humiliated.

He's right, of course. I am a black middle-class child from a mostly white, mostly working-class British suburb, and the Wu-Tang Clan are black working-class men from a black working-class American suburb. I have absolutely nothing in common with them other than the darkness of my skin.

He's wrong, of course. My skin is notably dark, dark even by the standards of most black people I know. It is stop-and-search dark, it is cross-the-road dark, it is don't-wear-a-hoodie-in-case-people-think-I'm-unfriendly dark, it is strangers-saying-tee-hee-all-we-can-see-of-you-in-the-evening-is-your-teeth dark. Most of these rappers are the same shade as me, and so I am Wu-Tang dark.

My teammate laughs at me, and what else can he do? I already take myself so seriously – for goodness' sake, I am still carrying around that briefcase – lighten up. And I can't explain that I am already terrified of lowering my guard and I am desperately looking around for examples of older black men who are reassuringly tough, but conflict in my parents' country scattered most of the older black men I personally know of, and so they are currently in exile elsewhere or are already dead. I can't explain to my teammate that I draw strength from these rappers as if they are my big brothers, because how weird would that sound? It sounds weird even thinking about it. But their music makes me feel brave, that if someone messed with me too much there might be the faintest chance that if Wu-Tang happened to be walking past, they might stop and sort them out.

YOU WANT TO TALK ABOUT CRIMINALS

I take a job at a local warehouse for a few weeks over the summer, packing solvents into boxes. The warehouse is a few hundred yards from the railway bridge, a short distance from where the man showed me the patchwork of swastikas inside his jacket. It's a quietly busy corner of town, one that is also home to a leading literary publisher and one of the largest publishers of pornography in the country. In my first few days I get chatting to one of the guys on the floor who has been there several years, and when he hears my accent, he asks what I am doing working in a place like this. I just need the money, I tell him, same as everyone else here. I get to know him a little better over the next few weeks and it turns out that for extra money he sells drugs to rich kids, including some students on the same boarding-school circuit as me. You want to talk about criminals, he tells me, how about the parents of some of these kids? Crooked, he says, shaking his head.

I don't ask too much about his other line of business because it seems rude, but I will later feel as if that was a missed opportunity. I have always wondered about the drug dealers who sell to my peers: how they go about their work; what they charge for what amount; where they meet and drop off their goods; how well they get to know their clients. Despite being stopped and asked for drugs many times in the street, it is ironic that I will know far less about them than my white schoolfriends. Unlike several of them, who appear to be connoisseurs, I will never know the slang for or the effects of every single different substance, and I will never learn exactly what an eighth is. Maybe some of this ignorance is aggressive and deliberate, another way of protecting myself from a world that I am terrified to inhabit.

By the time I reach adulthood I will have wised up a little, and I will enjoy pretending not to know which chemicals people are talking about. One weekend, as I am walking through a busy street in east London, two white girls will stop me and ask if I have some cocaine to sell them, using what they think is the most cool name for the drug. I will respond with a confused expression, and then, as I had hoped, I will receive a moment to savour: their utter disgust that a black man, of all people, would not know what that was. Ugh, one of them will say as they turn away. I will chuckle and continue walking.

THE END CREDITS OF RACISM

My suburb is so quiet that I begin to develop a theory: nothing exciting is allowed to happen in the towns that surround an airport. If this country is a feature film, then my suburb is the end credits, something to scroll through while I await the next burst of excitement. This is why I find it so strange that there is racial anger here. It doesn't seem to be an environment that is writhing with unrest, yet when I walk up the hill past the bank, I see a sticker on a set of traffic lights that says: *Pakis Beware, West London C18 in the area.* I know what a Paki is – despite being black, I've been called one of those before, but I guess that for some people any foreigner will do – but I don't yet know very much about C18.

I do some research and swiftly wish that I hadn't. C18 are Combat 18, the numbers 1 and 8 corresponding to the position of Adolf Hitler's initials in the alphabet, and they are exceptionally violent even by the standards of the far right. It's probably best that I don't bump into any of them.

I assess the situation and try to map out how far the racism extends across my town. This particular area seems to have its moments – I find the sticker across the road from where I saw the man with the jacket of patchwork swastikas – but where else should I be watchful? One spring I am revising in the library for my GCSE examinations, writing a set of notes from the encyclopaedia, when my pen gets stuck in a groove in the table; when I move the sheet of paper away to see what has obstructed it, I find that someone has carved a racist symbol into the desk: the initials of the National Front.

How does it feel, to know that so much hate has been sitting right here? In truth, it doesn't fill me with fear, it merely makes me more watchful. I have a look at some of the promotional materials that the far right have been putting up in my area and I see that they are printed in south London, so at least their headquarters are some way away. They are a short distance from where that black teenager was stabbed to death as he waited at a bus stop, a budding architect who was set upon by five white youths and who bled out as a helpless bystander held him. His death has a huge impact on me and many of the black kids who I know, because it proves that, in truth, there is no way to hide; that if I am black, I can live a life without blemish and they can still come for me.

I see them unsuccessfully investigate the murder of the black boy and they do a huge police report and conclude that the police force is institutionally racist, but they don't actually seem to punish anyone. How can an institution be that racist and still no one goes to jail? I think. Who have they found guilty then, the buildings? It takes them years to find the killers. I am lucky, though. I suspect that my town will only ever be the end credits for racism, but I take precautions all the same. For a few weeks one summer, when the mood seems to be turning just a little nasty, I walk the long way home, circling round the top of the road before descending towards my house. And soon enough I forget to do so, and it feels fine again.

MY SUPPOSED DIFFERENCE

A strange thing happens when I return to school at the beginning of my fourth year, which is that I am happy to see almost everyone, even the people I don't particularly like. Something has settled within me. I am secure in my presence here, my school uniform sits easily on my frame, I know what I am here to do. I ask a couple of friends, and they report that they are feeling the same thing. Maybe, as someone suggests when I raise this topic later, this is just what they call puberty?

So many things have changed for the better. For one, I am studying only the subjects I truly want to – medieval history, French, German and maths, a broad enough range to keep my brain engaged for the two years of my A-levels. I will never have to grapple with the harder aspects of physics or chemistry again. I have also grown a couple of inches, which means that, while I don't have a superbody, I am now slightly taller than one boy who looked down on me; we both notice this shift at once, and his small measure of power over me is lost.

Some of my friends and my teachers ask why I am not keen on studying English, which is by far my strongest subject, at either A-level or university. I lie to them. I tell them it's because I wish to go on to become a lawyer, and so I think that a law degree will be the best preparation for that career. The truth is that I am heartbroken at the thought of not studying English, but I believe that – as a dark-skinned man of foreign heritage – a law degree is a far more powerful piece of social currency in my country than an English degree will ever be. I have read the statistics, and I have made the following calculation: I understand that CVs containing names like mine, when presented to potential employers, are far less likely to attract interviews than similar CVs containing Anglo-Saxon names. I therefore decide to get the best possible qualifications that I can, in order to compensate for the fact that my potential employer might be put off by my supposed difference.

I am young, and therefore perhaps naive, but I can't yet understand why so many people with such astonishing creative gifts choose not to use them once they reach university. I see the greatest artists I have ever known, who genuinely seemed to love their craft, go on to become managers of many billions in assets – and I don't begrudge them that, I only wonder how much better the world's bookstores would be if they had their novels on their shelves. How many world-class authors and researchers have art and science lost to the boardrooms of corporate law firms?

Of course, I will soon understand the social and financial pressures that lead many people to make such choices. The only strange thing, I will see later, is that I was so obsessed with becoming a writer that I could not, in the end, have chosen anything else.

TWO BECOME ONE

I will never forget that walk home, trophy in hand. My teammate and I have just won the school debating competition, a title that the scholars' house has claimed year after year for most of the last three decades.

Fittingly enough, given the abrasive nature of the contest, the cup I am clutching used to be awarded to the best boxer in the school. Its silver surface is marked by a couple of dents, as if it was caught standing too close to one of those brawls. As I approach the front gate, I am euphoric.

I reflect on the final, which ended just a few minutes ago but whose memory already has a glow that will last for many years. I think of the confusion on the faces of my opponents in that last round; I remember them floundering as I produced an ace.

I knew before that evening that they were an exceptional team, as well read in the Classics as anyone I had encountered, but I also knew there was one thing they weren't expecting. Throughout the tournament I had heard many fellow students quoting ancient scholars, but I had never heard anyone quoting the Spice Girls or Wu-Tang.

And so, that evening, I work the most profound quotes I can find from the lyrics of popular musicians into my speeches. I muse upon the eternal compromise of marriage by asking people to consider what happens when 2 Become 1. I reflect upon the morality of the death penalty by noting Masta Killa's classic critique of it in Wu-Tang's 'Da Mystery of Chessboxin''.

My tactic has a disorientating effect on the opposition; it is as if I have turned up to a black-tie event wearing beach shorts and flip-flops. Bewildered by the form of my argument, they don't pay close enough attention to its substance.

And so it was, that in these august surroundings – the final was presided over by a high court judge, an old boy of the school – I was carried to victory by the arguments of five working-class kids turned pop stars.

I walk up the lane and through the front gate of my boarding house, its lawn nestling in the darkness beyond the soft porch lights. My housemaster opens the door and his eyes rush from my own to the trophy in my hands, registering surprise then a hint of delight. He smiles, and quickly beckons us in.

FASTEN MY ARMOUR

As the school's debating champions, my teammate and I are invited to a national tournament at a university a couple of hours away. When I turn up at the venue, I see a crowd of boys just like me from hundreds of other private schools, and for the first time I understand how boys like me must appear to the rest of the world.

The boys walk through the auditorium, a wave of dark blue suits and raised, uninterruptible voices. Even when they are filing in and looking for seats, their movements seem so assured, so purposeful. I have three debates in the first round, and I won't remember how many of them I lose, only that I am eliminated without much fuss. I never truly find my rhythm because the first sight of those boys unsettled me, they who talked in seamless sentences with no room for full stops and who accompanied their speech with a dramatic sweep of either hand, as if conducting an orchestra.

On my journey home, I don't tell my teammate that I feel relieved to have been beaten. I gaze out of the train window and I reflect on how nauseous I felt when we all arrived on that battlefield, but I had forgotten to fasten my armour and they hadn't.

SO MUCH BEAUTY IN HIM

Time and again, I see and hear how wealth can warp people's sense of morality. One schoolfriend tells me the story of his friend and his cousin who, on one holiday afternoon, went out for a drive in their sports cars. My friend's cousin, who was driving up ahead, crashed his vehicle and was badly injured, but when his friend arrived on the scene, he didn't help him out. He didn't so much as call an ambulance. Instead, he put his hand into his unconscious friend's pocket, took out his wallet, and spent thousands of pounds at a nearby mall.

On another occasion there is a boy who steals a huge sum of money from a boy in his own year, and when presented with the evidence, he shows no remorse. Later, as an adult, I will look online to see what he is up to now, and I will find that he is a vigorous defender of the sanctity of his own property, his disgruntled face glaring out from the pages of the local news.

Some might argue that money does not change people; it merely shows us what is already there. One day a wealthy friend tells me that he has servants at home, and that when he is there, he drops his clothes and never picks them up; that is for them to do. He asks me what I think of this, and before I respond I sense that he is testing me.

That's how you've been brought up, I reply, and he seems satisfied with that.

One boy, a member of a royal family, is one of the kindest people I meet at school. He has a rare warmth, always smiling whenever I cross his path, and I see why a place like this is a sanctuary for people like him; far from the pressures of home, where he will one day take the crown, he can go about his business unbothered. Three years after I leave, he will be murdered in a massacre of his family at his palace, and his final act is to beg his brother – the shooter, who also attended my school some time before me – not to kill his other relatives, but to take his life instead. When I hear of his act of courage, it doesn't surprise me at all. He was a human being with so much beauty in him.

PERHAPS THE FASCISM ADDS A BIT OF SPICE?

I think often of a schoolfriend of mine, one of the finest writers of prose I have ever seen. In my penultimate year, we win the chance to go to America for two weeks as part of a month-long exchange programme with an equally prestigious school, up near the north-eastern seaboard. My job, during the month-long programme, is to work with two editors from the American school and put together a magazine featuring artwork, poems and short stories from both of my student bodies. Our friendship is harmonious, and the job is a delight.

I am thoroughly proud of the magazine, which runs to well over a hundred pages and is published simultaneously on both sides of the Atlantic: it would take pride of place on the coffee table of any office. My friend, in a typically mischievous move, suggests that I include one piece of writing in the magazine that has absolutely no meaning. I agree, and we joke to each other that no one will actually have the guts to ask us what the hell it is doing there, and will instead have to conclude that it is simply far too deep for most minds to comprehend.

After we've hosted the Americans for two weeks, I

spend an idyllic fortnight with them in the US. I notice that even though the school is mixed, the boys and the girls sit on opposite sides of the lunch hall, separated by one huge table down the middle of the room. The boys themselves sit in different groups, separated as much by class as by race: the wealthy South Koreans, the rich white kids, the working-class Hispanic and black kids. My basketball game improves, and I develop an addiction to watching baseball and college football that lasts well over a decade.

There's a very nice girl in one of the years, far too attractive to be interested in someone like me, who I get talking to one afternoon, and she invites me round to her house for coffee. I don't go because I am busy working on my magazine, but a couple of days later, in the queue for one of the school's regular formal dinners, she calls my name and, my goodness, there she is in a ballgown of moonlight silk. She likes me, says my schoolfriend, and I tell him that no she doesn't, not like that; she is just being hospitable. Two days later, when I leave, I find a beautiful handwritten note from her in my letterbox, saying what a pleasure it was to meet me. I tell my friend about her note and he says, I think she liked you.

That weekend my American editors pull off a masterstroke of negotiation. They go to their headmaster and tell him, Look, we were treated so well in the UK, we can't fail to show our British friends a better time over here than they showed us. They arouse his competitive spirit, as they knew they would, and he presents the four of us with a generous sum of money. We promptly book two rooms in a four-star hotel in the middle of the nearest city, reserve a table for ten at one of its best fish restaurants, and in little time all the money has joyfully been spent. My friend pens a stunning summary of our visit; soaring, lyrical, riotously free. He writes it in a single sitting, a perfect first draft, the words pulsing on the page. Shortly afterwards, thanks to a sublime covering letter, he gains an internship at a prestigious advertising firm, and professional glory surely awaits him.

Three years later, to everyone's horror, he is diagnosed with cancer. Thankfully, his body and modern medicine manage to keep it at bay, and he comes to see me at law school, where I meet him for coffee and discuss his lucky escape. I thank him for the letters he sent me during his gap year, and I tell myself that I will be a better friend to him, that I will keep in touch with him as much as he keeps in touch with me. Few people make me joke away despair like him. I talk about the surge in racism I have been seeing in my home town, and he listens patiently, kindly, taking it all in, before encouraging me to look at the positives. Look, he points out, I'm always talking about how my home town is so boring, but maybe the racism adds another dimension to it. Perhaps, he suggests, pausing for comic effect, the fascism adds a bit of spice? His words hang there for a moment; he raises an eyebrow, as if intrigued; and then, my fear forgotten, I howl with laughter.

A few months after that, I get back to my flat one evening to see that I have received a letter. It is an invitation to my friend's funeral. His family did not have my contact details and so the letter has been forwarded to my address. His funeral took place a few days before.

Numb with horror, I get in touch with friends who attended, and I explain my absence. The church was overflowing with mourners, they tell me. The speeches brought everyone to tears.

But the cancer was gone, I protest. It was, they tell me, but it came back. My friend was only twenty-three and I wish I had told him how much I loved him, how much he inspired me. From now on, whenever I think of someone I love, I will get in touch to tell them just that. It is the very least that I can do in memory of this utterly wonderful human being.

THAT WILL NEVER WORK

Every so often the school will invite speakers to the main hall for an assembly, where they will give a twenty-minute presentation about their work to an audience of

500 boys. There is a wide range of guests, one of the most memorable of whom is a prominent anti-racism activist. I get to speak with him briefly afterwards, and he looks at me and then at the backs of the departing students. It is people like the ones here who can change things, he says. There is hope in his voice, and he makes me feel that maybe I could make a difference one day.

At other times my classmates will put on programmes of their own, elaborate comedy sketches as accomplished as those I'll see at festivals years later. This is the first time that I truly understand the power of satire as a weapon, how terrifying humour might be when turned in my direction.

The school assembly I remember best is a group of architects who come to explain their absurdly ambitious new project, a tourist attraction in the middle of the city, which looks like a slow-moving fairground ride. That will never work, I quietly scoff to my equally unimpressed neighbour. It will turn out to be the London Eye.

THE SCALE OF EVERYTHING

One of my favourite teachers gets in touch with me and says that he is leading a week-long trip of my fellow students to Russia, and that they have a couple of spare places. He wants to know if I would like to go – it will be a heavily subsidised visit, and so I will be able to go to Moscow and St Petersburg for a small sum. I ask my mother and she agrees at once, and so off I go. She offers to drop me at the airport, but I am gone before she has the chance, dragging my suitcase up that hill away from my road barely after 6 a.m., its wheels rattling over the gravel.

There is a particular reason why I am so desperate to flee my suburb. Because so much of my mother's money goes on school fees for me and my siblings, there is rarely any left over for holidays, and so I spend several of my summers watching all those planes from the nearby airport fly over the end of my road, envying their passengers. I gaze up as their smoke trails decorate the sky, wondering where they might be going. I drop my relatives at the terminal and wonder why they so often get to go through that gate, not me. As an adult, when I board a flight, it will feel magical, a privilege, because I know that so few get to soar. Once, I will go to America to see my cousins and I will feel as important as a rock star. I stare at the departure board in awe, quietly repeating the names of so many gloriously distant cities to myself: Shanghai, Bangkok, Dubai.

In fact, I will never lose my sense of wonder when I look at a departure board; each name upon it is a thrilling possibility, each one a city where my life could change for ever. As I grow older, I will hear people talk about borders with a sense of fear, of Europe as the bully and the enemy, but my instinct is always to explore. Maybe that was always in me, but years whiled away in a quiet suburb and within the walls of boarding school have given me an urge to roam that will be lifelong.

The trip to Russia comes at a time when its economy has been thrown open to all comers, and those with the most muscle, financial and otherwise, are busy claiming the spoils. When I arrive there, though, my untrained eyes only see fleeting signs of these dynamics.

We catch an overnight train from St Petersburg to Moscow, gazing out of the window at gloriously moonlit bodies of water and forests of endless depth. In Moscow I stay in a hotel whose floors become notably more grand as I ascend. I am staying about halfway up. One of my friends tells me he has been to the very top floor, where he says he saw several men with large bellies walking around with skinny girlfriends; I am not sure if I believe him, but I am far too scared to check.

Forewarned of the cold, I have packed the thickest clothes I can find, and step outdoors as carefully as an astronaut. Seemingly everyone is smoking the strongest cigarettes possible, with each packet far cheaper than it would be in my country; at the same time, American fast food is as expensive as a gourmet meal. Given its scarcity, perhaps it is a status symbol.

The use of public transport is a competitive sport, with people forcing themselves on and off the trains with notable vigour. The train stations don't have ticket barriers as such; instead, if I don't drop my token in the slot provided, a set of pneumatic pads emerge to punch me in the thighs. I walk around the city and am astonished by the scale of everything. The suburbs are a cascade of vast apartment blocks, and the spire of the state university seems to reach as high as low Earth orbit. If I lived here, I would feel engulfed.

I encounter a group of fellow students, teenagers from another Russian town, and some of them ask to take photos with me because they haven't met many black people before. At first I am perturbed, but my teacher says don't worry, don't take it personally, so I smile and agree, and I wonder if I will end up in a photo album somewhere. I hope I will. I get back in my coach and at a set of traffic lights, just before we move off, I think I flirt with a smiling girl in another bus, but then again, it could just have been eye contact.

Back at the hotel, I forget to listen to my teacher when he tells me to brush my teeth with bottled water, and so I end up losing my voice for a couple of days. One of the boys on my trip has a relative in this city and there is a rumour that she is very wealthy, but as usual no one explains exactly what she does for a living. At my school, it is rare that people actually talk openly about what their families do; it is assumed that we all belong in the room. Meanwhile, of course, the diligent will make a thousand discreet enquiries behind your back.

I learn barely any Russian, my vocabulary extending only to greetings, thanks and farewells. I do start to get a grasp of the alphabet, partly because I love the lettering. I can see why this country has produced so many great writers; this place has a size and complexity that lends itself easily to examination through novels.

As soon as I get back to school, I compose the best travel essay I can, laying it all out in longhand and walking it over to the editor of the school magazine, quietly confident that it is perhaps my best piece of writing yet. Oh my God, he says a week later, I am so sorry, I have lost it, and I never see it again. There is only one image I remember from it, just after I landed in Russia, where by the roadside I watched dogs in the snow, pawing at a few stray scraps of ice.

THE PERFECT HOME FOR ME

Each house typically appoints two house captains – one for the winter term, succeeded by one for the spring and summer terms – and in my final year, the first one to be appointed is me, followed by my best friend. The honour takes me aback. I always thought it would be my best friend, followed by another boy who also plays for the school's first rugby team; the latter boy seems to have more natural authority than me, more of the qualities that the school instinctively respects. I am very grateful for the position, though; I admire what my housemaster stands for, and I think that he has created a kind and protective atmosphere within the house.

I am also grateful for a far more selfish reason, which is that as house captain I am given a choice of large and beautiful rooms. I choose one away from the rest of my year, on the floor below. It's at the very corner of the house, with windows along two of its walls, and it over-looks the school grounds. It's a carefully detached place where I'll be able to do plenty of revision for my final year, and I'll seek out similar isolation when preparing for my examinations at university.

Thanks to the culture my housemaster has made, the younger boys seem happy to approach and joke around the boys in my year; they don't seem intimidated, and some of them even delight in calling me out on my bull-shit. Several of them are hilarious, and one reminds me of one of my cousins, rolling his eyes at my terrible jokes. To my silent amusement, one of them looks up to one of the boys in my year, looking at him adoringly whenever he walks past and then looking away whenever there is a risk of eye contact.

In my view, one of my housemaster's finest achievements will come ten years after I leave school. That's when there's my first reunion, the one I briefly attend on my way to a dinner, and I find that there are more boys there from my house than from any other house; a sign, I think, that he fostered a space where people from such different backgrounds could come together and feel relatively comfortable. I will always be thankful to him for helping me to go back out into the world with a sense of perspective, to retain a handle on what mattered most. I get the sense that he never fully bought into the school's pomp and privilege, which means that his house was in many ways the perfect home for me. My respect for him will only grow, and abundantly so, as time goes by.

THAT EXCLUSIVE CLUB

I hear the siren long before I see the boys. It is one of the final mornings of the term, a Sunday, and I am waiting for a church service; like most of my fellow students, I am in the common room of my boarding house, idly watching television.

That's when I hear the siren, that thrilling collective roar forced from the throats of a crowd of boys, echoing from the walls of the narrow passage that leads to the door of my house, and then the siren is inside my house, followed by those twenty boys, the school's stars, its senior prefects, and then they shove open the doors of the common room, here to welcome their next member. Oh, I think, they must be here for my best friend, but instead of him they turn to me, and lift me towards their shoulders in celebration—

Get out!

Everyone turns and my housemaster is standing in the doorway, his cheeks the colour of plum, his pupils boiling, his voice a blowtorch.

Get out!

The senior prefects sheepishly file out past my housemaster in silence, one of them passing me a pair of trousers as they go, and I am left holding the evidence of my new rank as some of my housemates step forward to congratulate me.

I have just experienced a ritual that is over two centuries old, the means by which I am invited to join the Eton Society, that exclusive club. Each year the school's senior prefects meet to elect twenty new members, and they have chosen me. The only problem is that I don't know why they have done so. It is meant to be the most glorious day of my life, but it is one of the most disorientating.

Why, I ask myself, have these people elected me? Most of them don't know me. I am pretty sure some of them don't even like me. I am shocked to discover that one boy voted for me, given that the only thing I can remember him telling me in the course of four years came in a heated sporting contest: they were the words *off* and *fuck*, and not in that order.

Why didn't they elect my best friend? He is good at everything – an outstanding leader, always humble, excellent at sport. Why didn't they choose one of my friends in another house – liked and admired by everyone who knows him, and someone who is accomplished in the classroom and on the stage?

One of the prefects in the year above sees my confusion and takes me aside, telling me not to mind all this, telling me that I belong. That morning, a little reassured, I walk into chapel wearing my new uniform, so that hundreds of fellow students can see who I now am: the same person, yet now somehow elevated. As I sit, some of them turn to me in surprise, several of them nod in acknowledgement, and one of them looks back at me and smirks, Nice trousers.

ENOUGH PEOPLE LIKE THAT

A few weeks into life as a prefect, I have mastered the art of the bow tie. At my fastest, I can assemble one in twenty seconds. I will never forget the tie's texture between forefinger and thumb, the light pockmarks across the thick, soft cotton, or how snugly it slides around my neck. When I fasten it, sensing the snap of the starch as the knot draws shut, I feel crisp, sharp, correct. I slide on my overcoat, flip its collar upwards, and then I float downstairs and out into the street. This will be the beginning of my love affair with jackets.

One of the privileges of being a school prefect is that the twenty of us are given our own room, a large, draughty affair with white walls and dark wooden benches along either side, a long dark wooden table down the middle, and a raised dark wooden chair at the furthest end, where, during meetings, the head prefect will sit.

I am given a sizeable budget for entertainment in that room, as well as a much-coveted subscription to a popular sports channel, but, despite the room being just round the corner from my beloved tuck shop, I barely visit it. This is too much comfort, I think – I haven't earned it.

I don't trust myself to indulge it – I am afraid my sense of self-regard will explode. I have just seen too many boys with erupting egos wearing this uniform before. I was elected to do a job, not to start thinking I am better than everyone. I view that room with the same suspicion that I will later view hard drugs: I never trust anything that is supposed to make me feel that good. If being a prefect here is such a high, then what is the low? How am I supposed to pay for it?

As a prefect, I not only wear a different style of trousers from everyone else, I am also allowed to wear a distinctive waistcoat, with a pattern of my choice. Most of the boys get at least one waistcoat specially made by a tailor in town. Some of them have humorous designs – one of my friends commissions one in the style of his favourite super-hero outfit.

Other boys have more traditional outfits, which seem to be based upon medieval symbols. I don't have a waist-coat made, which would have been fairly expensive in any case. I go to the prefects' room, find a second-hand one that is lying in the corner, and I use that one for the entire year, sending it for dry-cleaning every couple of weeks. This is my quiet form of protest – I am not going to fall in love with my own image; I am going to do the bare minimum necessary to be part of this group.

I later find out that the current prime minister of my country, the man who will one day take his country out of the European Union, was also chosen to be a school prefect. I wonder how he would have treated that room; I suspect that he would have draped himself over its fur-niture at every opportunity, mentioned it in conversation whenever he had the chance, taken it as proof that he was destined for the very greatest things.

Years later, looking at how I will struggle with my

self-confidence, I will have the uncomfortable thought that I wish I had spent more time in that room, that I had soaked it up, that I had drunk deeply from that well of ego.

Maybe there was something in that room that I needed – maybe part of being truly successful is walking through every door that I am offered and immediately believing that I own my surroundings. One evening I am at dinner with a friend and he looks at me, bemused. The funny thing about you, he says, is that it's like looking at a high-performance car where everything is in order – motor in perfect condition, the tank is full – but the car just won't start.

I have heard that type of thing about me before; it is a sentiment that has long haunted me. One of my classmates, seeing how well I played for my house, asked one of the school football coaches why I wasn't in a better team. My own argument was that I wasn't good enough – I wasn't the quickest, or the strongest, or the most skilful. But my coach said something different. He said that I had everything I needed but I just couldn't quite do it, and he didn't know why. In my less-certain moments, I fear that I know why. I fear that there are two types of people in life: those who walk proudly into the room, who assume that they deserve the keys to the world, and those who don't.

But then there are other times, more recently, when I think: No, I did the right thing. I was right to be wary of the strange gravitational pull that these offices seem to exert upon most people: like my housemaster, I was suspicious of them. I had seen one too many of the prefects in previous years carrying themselves with a little extra arrogance and was scared of becoming one of them. How could I have gone back to my home town carrying myself as if I was its emperor? Society has quite enough people like that.

Looking back, though, I wish that I had allowed myself to enjoy it a little more. I do have some friends who were also prefects in my year, and they were hardly people who let their narcissism run riot. Maybe, in future, I should just be less afraid of myself.

FOOTBALL IS ALL ABOUT LOVE

In the five years I have been at this school, it is the first time that my house has made it out of the first round of a sporting tournament. The next day I am due to play against a house full of elite athletes, whose starting team is drawn almost exclusively from the leading rugby players and footballers in the school. There is absolutely no one who expects us to beat them. Most people will be surprised if we are defeated by fewer than three goals. I sit at my desk and make a tactical plan. Their winger is one of the fastest sprinters in the school; their striker is one of its best finishers; their midfielder is not particularly skilful but has the best endurance of anyone on the field. Then I look at my own team and realise just how many advantages we have. Of the eleven of us who will take the field tomorrow, only three of us are in school teams of any description, which means that the opposition will know almost nothing about us. No one has seen them play.

The opposition won't know, for example, that while our left-winger has been judged too small and slow to get into a school team, he has a left foot that can land a pass up to forty yards away with exquisite precision. They won't know that our centre-forward makes up for his lack of speed and physical presence with a first touch as soft as a bed of moss. They won't know that our goalkeeper, still too short to have been noticed by the keenest scouts, has astonishing reflexes, that our left-back and our right-winger have useful changes of pace, that one of our centre-backs has two very good feet, or that our right-back, who doesn't care about much other than being a good person and his books, is one of the best defenders in one-on-one situations that I have ever encountered. I know all of this because of the countless games of five-a-side football we have played with them for the last three summers, during which we have all become aware of everyone's strengths and weaknesses and, most importantly, come to care about each other.

That next day, from the beginning of breakfast, through the morning's classes and on to the end of lunch, the match is all I can think about. That afternoon my teammates and I stroll to the fields together, past the flags and banners of the other teams and down to the pitch, where most of the boys from both houses are waiting by the touchlines. The whistle blows and it is only twenty or so minutes into the game, with the contest still scoreless, that our opposition begin to realise what we have done.

The night before, I realised that they had a far better midfield than us, and so my solution was simple: keep the ball out of the middle of the pitch at all times. So, instead of playing as a striker, I will play just in front of the defence. I will take the ball from my centre-back, play it to the left-winger, who will then hit a swift, swirling pass across the field to the on-rushing right-winger, who will place the ball into the perfect control of my striker, who will keep it while I sprint forward to join the attack. It is not an elegant strategy, but it continues working, mainly because our opposition can't believe that a team would be stupid enough to vacate the most important part of the turf. For a long time afterwards I will allow myself a smug smile at their confusion, standing about in the centre circle as the ball soared over their heads, left with so little to do that they may as well have unfolded a set of deckchairs. Inevitably, they begin to dominate the play, but by then, by half-time, my team's confidence is established; yes, the others may be faster, stronger and more skilful than us, but we are just as smart as them, if not smarter. After all, we are the academic house.

The longer the game goes without goals, the greater their frustration becomes, and then my team scores once – one of their defenders slicing the ball into his own net under pressure – and then twice – a penalty awarded for a foul on my centre-forward – and, though they manage a late strike of their own, they just cannot draw level. In the closing moments of the game, their striker rises to meet a high, curling cross with his head, making contact with the force of a well-slammed door, only for my goalkeeper to leap up and across and fling both arms towards the ball, swatting it just past his left-hand post with the tips of his fingers. The whistle blows and we have beaten them by two goals to one, maybe the most joyful sporting victory I've known in my five years here. That afternoon, when I tell my friends from other houses about the result, they look at me in disbelief.

That evening I am uncommonly exhausted; I have played hundreds of football matches but almost none as intensely as this. I fight harder for my housemates than for the members of any other team I have played for. I only realise at the end of my time at school that I am not so much a footballer as someone who cherishes the bonds that this sport provides; that is to say, I only play my very best when surrounded by teammates whose company I thoroughly enjoy. For me, in the end, football is all about love.

ABOUT A QUARTER

Of my year of 250 boys, about a quarter will attempt to get into Oxford and Cambridge. Despite the fact that a record number of us were admitted the previous year, there is a ridiculous yet persistent murmur among us that there is a bias against boys from my school, that perhaps our elite education will be a disadvantage.

It is possible to prepare for some subjects with mock interviews, but I am applying for law, so there is not much I can do – it is an aptitude test which changes from year to year and varies from college to college, so I have no idea what they are going to ask me about.

I am invited for an interview and I am not desperate to get into Oxford until I catch my train there. Then I see it. While my school's buildings are mostly brownstone, this university is acres and acres of sandstone, its colleges a succession of golden fields. I have to come here, I have to.

I spend the night before my interview trying to make my mind as sharp as I can, and I do so by working on several verbal reasoning tests. I do a couple of quick crosswords from the newspapers – I can't handle the cryptic ones – and then I head to bed. The next morning I have a written test – here are eight different people, here are some facts about their height, list them in order of height from one to eight – and an interview with three people, one woman and two men, one of whom is notably scarier than the other two. When he talks, the tip of his tongue looks so sharp that it could cut glass. The woman, the youngest of the three, seems friendlier, but I suspect that this is part of the act. I leave the interview room and as I descend the single flight of stairs, I am already preparing myself for bad news.

A couple of weeks later, when I am at home for my Christmas holidays, I am told that I have received an offer. My first reaction is to go into the downstairs toilet, look at myself in the mirror and slump my shoulders in relief. Thank God, I think, I do not have to go through life with the burden of being someone who went to a school like mine but didn't get into Oxford. Thank God. To have failed after having been given such privilege would have been unthinkable, a betrayal of an opportunity.

When I get back to school next term, I find that most of the other applicants have got offers, with the staggering exception of two boys in particular. Until this moment I could not have imagined there would be anyone out there cleverer than them. They will apply again the following year, gain admission to different colleges and go on to excel; everyone makes it in the end. Before we went for our interviews there was all this fevered talk of bias against our school, but after we have got our offers, I never hear anyone talk of bias again. Maybe we were just feeling entitled.

ACCORDING TO PLAN

I will never forget the moment when I learn that I have gained a place at one of the world's leading universities, subject to my achievement of certain exam results. For now, I am just happy that I will not have disappointed my family, but then my relief turns to fear. I am concerned by the high grades they have asked me to get. I have already earned a top grade in French – why did they not take that into account when assessing what they would need from me? I am worried because I have been struggling with two of my three remaining subjects; something odd happens to me when I do maths examinations – my confidence disintegrates, the symbols on the page before me become snakes and hooks. Those things happened to me in my first round of maths exams and now my marks are hovering just above a fail. The prospect of failing to get into Oxford after all this work is unthinkable. I have to do it somehow, I have to.

This is the day and the night that changes my life. It will be the period that I look to whenever I doubt my ability to pull through under pressure. I have history and maths examinations coming soon, the tests that will determine whether I get into university, and I need to revise. I am so afraid, and I get to my desk, and I remain there for twelve hours straight. I take no breaks. My concentration wavers at times, but I stay with it. I keep writing, dozens of pages of notes and calculations, absorbing every source, tracing out every equation. I will not fail, I will not fail. I finish at 4 a.m., the moonlight tracing its way across the far corner of my room, the lamp on my desk gazing fondly over me. To my right is a bag filled with jars of home-made peanut butter that my mother brought along as a surprise; it was her first visit to my boarding house during term time – she must have known I was worried. She must have taken time off work to bring that here. I will not let her down.

I receive my examination results, and something extra-ordinary has happened. It is in the papers that I found most difficult that I have scored my highest marks. My lowest mark for a mathematics paper is 90 per cent and my highest mark is 93. I score 100 per cent for my history dissertation. I am safe, I am safe.

I go into town just so I can walk about and enjoy the euphoria. I start to receive messages of congratulations from members of my family, but amid them is one different form of communication that I will never forget, which reminds me that even, or especially, those who are nearest to me by blood will not always share my best interests. One of my cousins picks up the phone to me to check how I have done, and when I tell her of my success she simply says, Some things do not go according to plan. I am so shocked that I cannot ask her what she means, but I know what she means – I always have – which is that the unfairly privileged education I have been given has made people root against me.

Years later, another cousin will tell me that, Hey, you know what, when we were growing up, I used to hate you. Though I will understand his envy, since I was given an opportunity that he wasn't, it doesn't make his words any less painful. I am more wary of him for years after that, just in case some of that hate is still there.

A TONE OF CRUELTY

A few months from the end of my time at school, I do one of the most childish things I have done in the entire five years I have been there. It is this: every time my housemaster does anything mildly irritating, I and most of the other boys in my year go to a corner of the sixth-form common room and make a small marking on the wall in black felt tip, a symbol mocking his name, as if we are prisoners confined to some dungeon. At first there are just a few, but then they rapidly multiply, and what began as a light-hearted joke eventually assumes a tone of cruelty.

One day my housemaster walks into the very furthest corner of the common room and he finds the markings, the mean caricatures of him. We each confess to having put them there. He seems hurt and utterly disappointed, and I am disappointed in myself too. It is a formative experience for me: from then on, I will check myself whenever I feel that I am going for cheap laughs at the expense of others. It is a classic example of what can happen when young men get carried away with a joke at someone else's expense: it is one of the most painful and powerful lessons I will ever learn.

AH, THAT'S WHERE THEY WENT

The far right are seemingly so confident that they are going to have political success in my home town that they put not one but three parties on the ballot in my constituency: the British National Party, the National Democrats and the National Front. The first two are more likely to be the type of people I might hear on the radio and see on the television, while the Front tend to be a street gang, far more interested in fighting it out than talking it out.

For a moment I am concerned that they might put in a strong showing in the general election, but when the results come back, they are utterly humiliated. They only narrowly finish with a higher combined total of votes – 462 – than the Monster Raving Loony Party, which ends up with 396. By comparison, the winning candidate – from the Conservative Party – acquires just over 16,000 votes, almost 4,000 more than his second-placed rival for Labour. The winner is a much-loved local businessman who runs a renowned furniture store, one of whose rugs adorns the floor of my room at school. For years that rug, its imitation-Persian patterns tastefully matching the red decor of its surroundings, is my most expensive purchase: it cost me the princely sum of £47.

For a long while after that, no one will really talk about the far right. Their ideology is like malaria: it strikes intensely for a short while, leaving the people feverish, then retreats, apparently eliminated, but is truly just biding its time. I will remember their meagre vote count decades from now, how I thought back then that their threat had been conclusively snuffed out. At the time, I won't draw a connection between their failure and the vigorous effects of the local anti-fascists to remind everyone just what these parties stand for. I won't consider that the anti-fascists have successfully exposed what lies at the root of their political outreach, which is violence, segregation and hate: I will assume that the electorate came to this judgement all by itself.

After university, while training as a lawyer in the City, I will even end up living in an area that was once a far-right stronghold, and I won't experience any incidents of racist abuse while I am there. What I will notice while I am there, and what greatly unsettles me, is the tone of the posters for the Conservative Party's general-election campaign. I see them on the bus on my way to work, and the most memorable one states that it is not racist to put limits on immigration, and then asks if I am thinking what they are thinking. I am disturbed by this because I understand immediately that the poster is not addressing me – it is attacking me, and people like me. Anyone with my heritage knows very well that there are, and always have been, limits on immigration, and that it has long been a tactic to say that people like me are here to invade and then bleed dry the British state, slashing at it with our knives, dragging out its steaming guts with our greedy hands.

When these posters are released, they are met with fury and the Conservative Party suffers in the polls as a result. The country's economy is surging, many people are doing better financially than they did before; it is unclear why the Conservatives have chosen this as a platform for attack. Some are reassured by this backlash, but I see it differently. I saw those posters every day as I was getting one of the world's most coveted professional qualifications, following years of hard study and a spotless criminal record. The message I took from them was that, no matter what I achieved here, there would always be someone in a senior political position who was ready to try and put me in my place. That was the subtext of the poster campaign, and I knew it because I had seen its tone somewhere before – in the flyers that the British National Party once posted through my door. At times I will wonder what happened to the far right and then I will look at those posters and eventually I will think, Ah, that's where they went.

SPACE TRAVEL

Until I am nineteen years old, the concept of having a girlfriend will be as strange to me as space travel. For the most part, this isn't a problem for me – from a distance, it is an enterprise that looks stressful. By far the hardest thing, in my experience, is maintaining my confidence when I approach someone. One afternoon I attend a friend's birthday party, one of the rare occasions where I see someone from my school during the holidays, and I meet a girl there who I find so attractive that when I look in her direction my lungs fill with a vacuum and I cannot speak. Unable to handle her gaze, I come up with the brilliant strategy of angling my head away from her and pretending to address my whole group of friends while actually aiming my best anecdotes towards her. This plan works fairly well until, having heard me joke about something I did wrong, she gently laughs and says, Wow, that must be the first time you have failed at something in your entire life.

My God! What do I say to that? My tongue has become a length of wool, suddenly stripped of all moisture, muscle and movement. I manage to start a sentence, but the only way I can complete it is with an apologetic cough. Before her friendly intervention my confidence was unshakeable but now that it is actually time to interact with her, my self-esteem has drifted away on the city breeze. I barely speak for the rest of the party, and when I go to say goodbye to her, I think she looks slightly baffled.

By the end of my first term at university I am much better in this respect. I have worked out that when I have decided to talk to someone I like, there is a time lag of about ten seconds before my ego tells me that this is a terrible idea. So just speak up quickly, I think, and you'll be fine; get those words out of your mouth before your self-esteem has a chance to collapse.

FREE OF ITS ORBIT

When I leave school, we are each asked to submit a page to the yearbook. My submission is a collage of some photos of me set against the backdrop of a flyer from a far-right political party. Someone had delivered that flyer to my home by hand during the local elections, which means that my quiet neighbourhood was a place where a white supremacist felt comfortable walking right up to my door. I found it on the mat later that day, thankful that they apparently didn't know a black family lived there; I know that there is a street in my town, over towards the canal, where black families have had dog faeces posted through their letterboxes.

The collage I send is a humorous one, in which I manage to cut and paste the text of the flyer so that it looks like the wording from a tourist brochure, but it is also my way of saying: This is an element of my life away from the comfort of school, this is why I am sometimes so guarded. I look at the collage afterwards and it reads as if it is not only a farewell to my school but to the entire environment that surrounds it, that even then I was beginning to vigorously pull free of its orbit.

A few weeks before I leave my school, I have a slightly self-indulgent conversation with one of my housemates, looking back on my time there. We both hope we have made a good impression on the other boys in our year, and I assure my friend that he has. His verdict on me is kind and considered; it leaves me feeling a little sad, but satisfied. When people look at you, he says, they'll think he was a nice guy, but I never really got to know him. And, he adds, I think that's kind of how you like it.

I FAINTLY REGRET

At the end of my final term I meet with the other prefects for a farewell dinner in west London. We all somehow stuff ourselves into the basement of a restaurant, and it is a very pleasant evening; it is a few years before I will start to drink, a fact which, when looking back at the quality of wine on offer that night, I faintly regret. I am the first to leave that gathering, since I have by far the furthest to travel home, and the last train is due to depart in about half an hour.

As I make my way out, one of the boys – with whom I did not get on all that well – says goodbye, and his tone is strikingly kind, which surprises and moves me. He wishes me the very best, and he genuinely means it. In that moment, I feel quite wistful. I look around the room and I briefly wish I had allowed myself just to enjoy it all a bit more, to dissolve myself in that world for a short while, to indulge in its traditions. But the moment is just that, because I know that if I had done that, then I would have fallen in love with a world that would never truly be my own. And so I thank the boy quickly, and then I am up the stairs, out into the street and away.

PART THREE
REUNION

A TICKET TO PROSPERITY

For years after I leave school, I will be attacked by shame. The sensation will rush over me, a blast of cold air after I have thrown open my front door to a winter morning. I feel it whenever I doubt whether I have made the best of my education, which is often. My schooling was a ticket to prosperity, and yet I ripped it to shreds.

It is only after years of not having made much money that I will realise how much that money – or, more accurately, the pressure to earn money – has been a motivation. I have never been particularly materialistic – I have never gone past a large house or nice car and thought, I would desperately like one of those – but I do have a growing sense of duty, and therefore of embarrassment. There is a constant inner voice telling me that the eldest son of refugees should have done more than this to help his family financially. I never craved wealth for myself, and it is not too often that I am pressured by my relatives to acquire it for their sake, but I could have done so and helped them out.

There are times when I think that if I had known the shame would be so aggressive, then I might have made different choices. But then I look at so many of my peers who went from school to university, and then on to long careers in the City, and I think, But I was just never like them. I was always one of the odd ones out. I went through those same interview processes and sat in those same offices, and yet a different and less lucrative life always called to me. I will never forget the way one class-mate once looked at me thoughtfully, as if having observed me a while from a distance, and then said, You do kind of go against the grain, don't you?

I would sit in class and wonder, Why is it that so many of the most brilliant creative minds of my generation, the ones in their teens who wrote essays and editorials remi-niscent of great, long-dead writers, are going off to do jobs that just make themselves and other rich people richer? What are they doing, with all that skill they have in their pens and within their souls, to shape the world for the better? Why don't they care more?

There are other times – far more than I am proud to recount – when I wonder what is wrong with me. Why is money not personally so important to me? Why have I routinely rejected opportunities to make it? Why, when in the midst of an atmosphere that encouraged me to do so – surrounded by the children of merchant bankers and other assorted financiers – did I not simply ask around and see if I could get some work experience one summer?

But then I remember how focused I was. How I never asked for anything then and I rarely ask for anything even now; how I wanted to earn my way, not to be a charity case. There is a severe stubbornness in me, a firm sense of purpose and a refusal to compromise that may, at its root, be vanity.

THAT ANGRY BLACK GUY

When I am in my second year at university, I bump into a friend from school, and I catch up on the few years in between. At one point in the conversation my friend says, I know, there's this story about you, this story they used to tell about you at school.

Ah, what's that? I ask.

Apparently, you were on a bus in your home town and you saw that a white man was listening to one of your favourite rap groups. And apparently you went over to the white man, pulled his headphones out of his ears and told him, You shouldn't be listening to that, that's black people's music.

What? I say. I never did that.

No, no, my friend says, sounding anxious, when they

told me that story, they said you were a legend for doing it.

It's a terrible story, I say. And in any case, it's not true.

Hours later, I am still angry. The story is so obviously false, and I know where it originated from. There was a famous rapper who was rumoured to have told white people she didn't want them listening to black people's music, and somehow that rumour has been ascribed to me. I am trying to work out why I am so upset, and finally I get it – because there are many people who saw me as that guy, as that angry black guy, the type who would storm up to a stranger in public and violate their space. Not for the first time, I wonder, What was the point? If people thought I was that guy, I may as well have gone and been that guy anyway. Most painfully, I realise that my friend who proudly told me the story believed that it was the kind of thing I would do, and that he, too, did not really know me at all.

INDIFFERENT TO THE DESPERATION

It is grim to witness some of the school's former students with little apparent compassion for so many of their country's occupants. I once watched them in awe in debating chambers and on televised university quiz shows as they destroyed their intellectual rivals, casting them aside with their superior wits. Now I read and watch interviews where they can barely contain their contempt for people who are poorer and less gifted, where they defend policies that take blowtorches to the budgets of local communities. I wonder how they became that, or whether this is who they always were.

Each time I see a leading Conservative politician from my school in the news, either the ones who were in the year above me or those who were there a generation before, I note that they always seem to have the same brutal outlook, the same ruthlessness towards public-spending cuts. They seem indifferent to the desperation of disabled people claiming benefits; they swat aside the latest poverty statistics as if they were weak retorts in a sixth-form debating chamber. For them, maybe politics is tennis, and every unhappy fact is thrashed away with a single-handed backhand. Or maybe, for some of them, poor people are merely figures on a spreadsheet, people whose pain to them was never truly tangible. Why aren't they more representative of the range of people I knew at school? Surely most of my classmates would never have signed off on these endless years of austerity, this devastating economic experiment that has crushed much of the country.

But then I think, Hang on, how naive. The boy who was our head prefect, someone I could not have admired more at school for the way he conducted himself, crafted the same economic policies that the United Nations' poverty expert would later describe as harsh and uncaring, as punitive, mean-spirited and often callous. Almost every schoolfriend whom I have seen express a political view on social media has been Conservative. And why wouldn't they be? This world works for them just as it is. It provides them with living standards and a basic level of comfort that are unimaginable to most people. Why the hell would they want to change that? Both of my boarding schools were overwhelmingly right-wing environments; the two newspapers most often lying around, by a significant distance, were the *Daily Telegraph* and *The Times*. When, at prep school, someone mentions the name of Malcolm X, the school matron dismisses him as *that horrible man*. This was the world from which these politicians emerged – from which we all emerged – and it proves that you don't have to be cruel in your daily life to enact policies with cruel effects. You merely have to absorb the mantra, fed to you forever by such surroundings, that you must, above all else, be fiscally conservative.

So why *wouldn't* many of my contemporaries vote for austerity? It's so much easier to deprive your fellow voters if you've never paid careful attention to their suffering. And a key problem for too many people from my school is that they've never really seen widespread poverty. They have read about it, and maybe even seen it on their gap years or trips abroad, but they don't really believe in it – that is to say, they largely think it is something you can elevate yourself out of, if you are just a little smarter, work just a little harder.

Of course, several classmates have endured personal tragedy: riches do not make anyone immune from the most horrifying of losses. Yet as a whole, as a class, they have endured. The reason we can hold such grand anniversary celebrations every ten years is because we are utterly certain that there will be so much to celebrate. We are absolutely sure that most of us will be affluent, if not wealthy. On the whole, hard times do not happen to us, while for most of the rest of society hard times are the norm.

DON'T FORGET US

There is a boy in my home town to whom, by my standards, I have started to grow close. A couple of years younger than me, he is always friendly, always restless. One of the last times I speak to him, just as I am about to leave university, he has received a conviction for vandalism after he was caught spraying graffiti in the wrong part of town. Whenever he gets in trouble, it seems to result from boredom.

One summer I go down to the basketball court and the boy is there, leaning against one of the fences. It is only a few months before I move out of the area to London, never to return, but I don't know that yet; he can already sense it, though. He asks where I've been, he hasn't seen me in a while, and I say I've been in the States, doing an internship at a law firm there, that they might offer me a job. He is impressed and he goes quiet for a little while. I see you doing your stuff and working hard at that school, he says eventually, and I'm just here dossing around, with low confidence.

I am startled by his frankness. He's not the kind of person who is given to admitting any kind of weakness; he's too cool, too quick-witted for that, cruising around in his classic tracksuits and his impossibly spotless white trainers. I am still processing this burst of honesty when he says something that breaks my heart.

When you leave, he says, please don't forget us.

He doesn't have any idea what I will go on to do with my life; he is only sure that it will involve living in and travelling to places far more thrilling than the one where we both grew up. It is clear to him that I am on the edge of adventures while, as far as his life's journey goes, he seems to have accepted that this is his final stop.

A little while later I am so affected by this story that I mention it to a fellow writer, and when I finish telling it she nods matter-of-factly. Of course that's how he felt, she says, and she sounds surprised that I am surprised. There are some people, she tells me, who are done at eighteen, it's over for them. I can't believe this, or maybe I just don't want to admit that a black boy with a criminal record in a small town could have had the fight permanently knocked out of him. For all my struggles with self-confidence, I am always reassured by the knowledge that I have been raised in an education system where everyone makes it. I have never forgotten the thorough and trembling shame in his eyes as he confessed to low self-esteem, and I never will.

OFTEN TOO LATE

The old-boy network is based on the concept, which seemed benign to me at the time of attending Eton, that most, if not all, people who went through that same formative experience are fundamentally decent beings. When any of them make the news, be that in the tabloid gossip pages or for their poor political judgement, my reflexive tendency is at first to see them through the prism of what they were like at school, when they, like me, were just awkwardly finding their way.

The old-boy network is therefore, on the whole, much

more subtle than offering someone a plum job. It is the instinct to stick up for someone you barely know, the watered-down criticism, the scrutiny turned away at a crucial moment. It is the belief when you see people making bigoted statements that they are somehow better than that, that they are merely making a gaffe, when all available evidence indicates that they are not. This belief can be just as dangerous as active support of bigotry, because it results in years of failing to acknowledge a developing threat, of patronising others when they tell you that there really is a problem.

I think specifically of the moment when a man in his mid-fifties, startled at the rise of a far-right politician he knew during his private-school days, pens an anonymous letter to a national newspaper, revealing that this politician had held fascist views in his late teens. It has taken this man decades to speak out, and by the time he has done so the politician in question is already too well established in his career to be affected.

The reason the man has not spoken out till now is partly because of a sense of loyalty: because he knew the politician as a friend, and therefore hoped he might turn out for the better. But it rarely works out that way: the demagogues pursue their destiny, and their peers either stay silent or cheer them along. By the time many of us unlearn the impulse to defend our tribe at any opportunity, it is often too late.

TO MAKE ETON SPEAK

One day, a news item seizes my attention. The head-master of my former school is advertising a scholarship scheme in the country's most popular newspaper, the *Sun*, in the hope that working-class parents will read about it and encourage one of their sons to apply. One of the scholarship students featured most prominently in the paper, his smiling face peering out gratefully from the pages, is the child of African refugees – the same group of people that that same newspaper, not long previously, had described as cockroaches while they were drowning in the Mediterranean.

The headmaster of my school seems unaware of the tabloid's hypocrisy. There is some criticism of my school's decision to make a partnership with this paper, but it soon subsides. It is then that I notice that my school has a very effective way of dealing with any negative press that it receives, and that is the use of silence.

If Eton has any devastating weapons against its opponents, then the greatest of them is its ability to leave things unsaid. For an institution so often in the news, it issues remarkably few press statements, thus suffocating the controversy. In this context, it is therefore a great achievement for the media to make Eton speak.

My school does not like talking about itself, and this is a lesson that many, if not most, of its students have absorbed. I remember several occasions where boys from my school are asked where they studied, and with a quiet and knowing pause they reply, Somewhere near Slough. It is a feigned innocence, an act of tactical embarrassment, beneath which often lies a quiet sense of supremacy.

I keep reflecting upon what Eton doesn't talk about. I look a little more into the history of some of my school's most famous alumni, several of whom made their wealth from the enslavement of human beings, and I wonder why I was not taught about this part of their history. I know by now that slavery was not simply something that everyone just accepted back then, that for hundreds of years it was vigorously resisted all over the world. Slavery was an abomination, and the families of many of those with whom I shared a classroom have long profited from it.

I wonder what is in the family photo albums of so many of those with whom I attended school. I think about my great-grandfather, a man my mother often discusses fondly, and I think about how history is so close. And then I think about that boy in my year who said with a sneer that his great-grandfather was a slave driver, how when I remember these words the blood of those enslaved people again becomes fresh on the ship's deck.

I look at a register of those who owned human beings and see that a large proportion of names there are people who once attended my school. It reminds me that the history of the British Empire is intimately connected with the history of Eton, and yet the latter is notably quiet about the most notable element of the former. I read about Operation Legacy, the twenty-year process during which Britain destroyed documents that detailed the most horrifying aspects of its empire, just in case citizens of its former colonies should see them. Those documents, describing countless acts of torture and murder across a range of countries, were confined to archives, bonfires and the depths of the sea.

I wonder how many former students of my school took part in that process, even while they and much of the rest of the world were raised to believe that the British stood, above all, for the concept of fair play. I keep thinking about those surnames, those estates, that wealth, built upon the cracking and the crushing of black flesh and bones.

When, years later, people criticise Eton to me, I at first find myself defending the kind people I knew there, the patient teachers and the charismatic pupils. But then I step back and I understand that these people are not attacking those acts of kindness; they are striking at something bigger and much more important than that. They are attacking my school for its role in moulding the leaders of a society which for millions of people is unfit for purpose. They are attacking its failure to acknowledge that role.

When we see our boarding schools receive criticism in the media, our first instinct is often to say, But I worked so hard for all that I have. Well – we did and we didn't. Yes, we may have got outstanding grades, but the access that we were granted as a result of those grades, the doors opened in social circles by the mere mention of the name of the place of our education, is simply something that cannot be earned. It is just not possible.

I think about how naive I was. I knew one boy at school whose family had made money through dubious means, and I thought, One day, when we're both old enough, when he has more influence in their business, I'll talk to him about how he can make positive changes. I was true to my word, but years later – when the time came for that conversation and I raised the subject with him – he brushed me aside. He barely acknowledged what I was saying, and I have not been in contact with him since.

If I have learned anything about Eton and the boarding-school world more generally, it is that true and positive change is highly unlikely to occur from within. The benefit of maintaining things just as they are is too considerable, the questions to be asked about the sources of colonial wealth are too uncomfortable. I will realise this when, in the middle of the Black Lives Matter movement and during a vigorous international discussion about Britain's role in the slave trade, Eton's headmaster speaks, and it is not to talk about what part his school's alumni played during the centuries of colonialism, or what could be done to educate future generations about that. Instead, he merely chooses to apologise to a black student who experienced racism while he attended Eton. The apology is a disappointingly small response to the grandest of questions, but it should not have been unexpected. It is one thing for an institution to admit that it may have got some things wrong, but another to consider in full public view whether it is fundamentally a force for good.

When I was still at Eton, there was one question we continually asked each other: *Would I send my son to Eton?* We asked each other this because even while we were there, we knew that this was no ordinary school, that its name contained an unusual power. My own answer was no, because I knew even then that it was a place where a boy's connection with reality could be all too easily severed. Over time, though, I have thought that we were asking ourselves the wrong question, that we should have wondered instead why one institution should have all this influence. I look at the school's motto, 'May Eton Flourish', and I think, It is not right that you flourish, and will continue to flourish, at the expense of so many others.

THE GOLDEN RULE OF THE CLASS SYSTEM

I can tell the middle-aged man is wealthy within seconds of beginning to speak to him. I meet him, a business acquaintance of a relative of mine, in a pub one afternoon. The first thing he does is to assert – quietly, carefully and with devastating modesty – who exactly is paying whom.

Do you and my relative work together? I ask the man, making conversation.

No, says the man, he's actually sort of done a few things for me.

His accent is that of someone who went to a school like mine, yet, as we later talk about the state of the country and I mention the social and economic inequality that we can ascribe to the class system, he informs me that the class system no longer exists. This is what I should have expected from him. The golden rule of the British class system is that you absolutely cannot talk about the existence of that which benefits you the most.

It does exist, I tell him, though of course we both know this. It is stronger than ever, I say. Really? he says, giving a perfect impersonation of someone who is genuinely startled.

Next, he is intrigued to learn where I went to school. This information is not offered to him by me, but by my relative, perhaps in the hope that it might impress him.

You're in the City? he asks.

No, I reply, I'm a journalist.

Hmm, he says. Great use you've made of your expensive education.

I don't react to that, because he is my relative's client and I do not want to do anything that costs him business, but I think, Ah, this is like being back at school again: the sparring, the search for insecurities. It is a good thing that I have already put on my mask. He asks where I went to university and I tell him. It turns out that he could have gone to Oxford too, actually; it is just that he chose to go somewhere else. Ah, I think, they all say that.

He is evasive about the nature of his own work and refers to earning money as making a few pennies here and there. After he leaves, my relative comes up to me and says, You do realise that man's absolutely loaded? I laugh. I have a radar for that stuff, I say, even though this man didn't exactly make it hard to detect: everything he said was a form of attack. Each sentence was a powder-keg of passive aggression. Later I look online for any trace of this man's name; and of course, given the furious invisibility of so much of the country's wealth, there is little to none.

INVISIBLE WALLS

Despite all of the years I spent at boarding school, I never quite managed to feel at ease with the invisible walls in the wider society that surrounded it. There always seemed to be these social borders in certain places. I go to a private members' club for a schoolfriend's leaving party, and on my way through the entrance – even though I know exactly where I am going – I make sure to stop and introduce myself to the security guard, just in case he is surprised to see an unfamiliar face going past, and by unfamiliar I mean black. The guard thanks me courteously for my manners, and I proceed. A few minutes later, another black man arrives at the party, visibly furious, and I immediately know why. You walked straight through security, didn't you, I say. I did, he says. Without saying hello to the guard, as if you belonged here. Yes, he says, and this guy, he followed me all the way across the lawn and into the hall. Ah, I said, not without sympathy. We look around us at the party. There are plenty of people who aren't members of this club, who have walked through that same entrance without so much as a glance from security. The only difference is that they are white and therefore look as if they belong here, and we two don't.

In time, I learn how to navigate these invisible walls. For one thing, I know that my accent is a visa. When I enter a place where the presence of someone who looks like me is uncommon, I make sure to open my mouth as soon as possible, so that they will be reassured by this indicator of my social class. It is comparable to the reaction I get when I am travelling through some parts of Europe and I produce a British passport – I am suddenly not one of those Africans but one of Us, a member of the Western world, an infinitely safer prospect.

I AM THEREFORE DISMISSED

The process of assessment is so quick, and almost painless, as if the man is taking a sample of blood from the tip of my finger. I have just met him at a party in Amsterdam and he is working out whether I am of sufficient social value to continue acquaintance. Though we are both in our mid-thirties and have lived away from the UK for some time, he can hear from my accent that we went to similar boarding schools. Where did I go, he asks. I tell him, and he tells me that he went to Harrow, the rival place. We exchange half-hearted teasing, and then he presses on with his assessment. It quickly becomes clear that he is more interested in who I may be connected to than who I actually am.

Do you know so-and-so? he asks. Yes, I say, I played sport with him, but I haven't seen him in years. And do you know so-and-so? he asks, referring to a friend of mine whose family runs a large company. I do know him, though not particularly well, but I don't admit that: I suddenly don't want to make it that easy for him. The man looks disappointed. A few minutes later a woman arrives at the party, her dress shimmering as if she has just floated down from some penthouse, and though he does not know her, he greets her with an arm very low around her waist, his head leaning towards her and away from me, his gesture the full stop on our conversation. Whatever he was looking for in me, some kind of foothold or rung leading elsewhere, he did not find it; I am therefore dismissed, and happily so.

A CREATURE OF MOMENTUM

Later, when I move to mainland Europe, people will ask where the floppy-haired British prime minister came from, how such a man could ever hold high office, and I will tell them truthfully that I saw his election coming ten years ago.

The person to whom I made this prediction is living even further from the United Kingdom than I am, and that is possibly no accident. Ten years ago we talked at length about much of the media and the electorate's resentment of immigrants, about much of the country's willingness to brush aside the damaging social and economic policies by successive governments, and concluded that this mix of bigotry and unseriousness was tailor-made for the current prime minister to take advantage.

But where did the prime minister come from? People closer to his social circles inexplicably express surprise, as if they were fish suddenly startled to discover that they are surrounded by water. They didn't see him coming because some element of him was always there. You could hear his style of fact-free bluster at any private-school debating society. You could see his confidence preening out from any photo of private-school prefects. You could find his amoral swagger, hidden in a cartoon-ish cloak, in just about any fringe political society at the universities of Oxford or Cambridge. The only thing that made the prime minister unique is that he combined all of those assets within one frame.

We could never tell that he would be in power one day, say my peers. These are the same people who confidently predicted that, when the American president was elected, the natural checks and balances of his nation's political system would limit his abuses of his office. These people all too quickly forgot that their own vigilance was part of the UK's checks and balances, that their refusal to speak up at crucial times was, in its own way, just as important.

Such people need to understand that the ego is a creature of momentum, that obstacles must be placed in its path at certain points, otherwise it will continue to grow, and there will come a point when it is unstoppable. I remember friends telling me, just after I had left university, that they were on reasonably good personal terms with a budding politician who was already openly showing far-right beliefs. What are you doing about it? I asked, and one of my friends shrugged, Oh, he is a fascist, as if fascism were merely a difference of opinion, like supporting a football team, and then went back to watching his ascent. My friends seemed not to realise that bullies like that didn't need their support; that, for them, the silence of their peers is the same as a standing ovation.

How could he have become the leader? they ask, and that is perhaps the wrong question; the right question, perhaps, is how could he not? In a political system closed to all but a few, with the same few names in constant rotation and with no apparent consequences for grave failure, such an individual was eventually bound to get his chance. Many of the same people apparently horrified at his coronation, and who describe him as an anomaly, mostly share his world view; it is just that he is less polite about it. The prime minister may be outlandish in his speech and appearance, but he is not an outlier.

I hear of several fellow old boys from my school – a few years older than me, from the same generation as the prime minister – who have watched the unfolding political situation in my country with horror, and who are asking themselves what they could have done to prevent it. They are asking whether they could have spoken up more at certain times, to discourage people who they felt might do serious damage if they were elected. As much as these old boys may beat themselves up, they may be in danger of missing what I feel is the key point: that the fate of a nation should not come down to whether the nice guy or the nasty guy in your class ends up as prime minister. Power should simply not be held so tightly by one group, being passed around the same circle of individuals as if it were a joint on a night out.

All the same, perhaps those old boys did see this coming a long way off, knowing that the politicians who they knew in their schooldays would remain essentially unchanged as adults. The obvious truth is that if such boys stay within that boarding-school world – hanging out with the same small collection of characters they grew up with at work and on holiday, and never really looking beyond that – then their world view doesn't alter all that much. Since I attended my school, the fees have more than trebled in just twenty years, meaning that they would now be unaffordable to someone like my mother, and that most of the boys there will be drawn from an even narrower segment of society. While my school is more likely than ever to produce more prime ministers, it is grim to think that the journey I took – a full five years there at 50 per cent of the fees – is no longer possible for boys like me. The only option would be a sixth-form scholarship, which means I would only get to spend two years there, at most. The message it would send to someone like me now, from my social and economic background, is that mere academic excellence is not good enough. Beyond that, though, there is the more important question of whether the act of obtaining an outstanding education for your children should be a financial assault course. For my part, I think that it should not.

THE NEXT WAVE OF MONEY

I catch up over drinks with a couple of schoolfriends I haven't seen in years. They've been living on the other side of the world and have been following my writing; they have happy home lives and fulfilling careers, about which they fill me in with joy. Talk turns to gossip about other boys in our year. They tell me that so-and-so is making many millions of pounds a year, and I am surprised by that. I know plenty of brilliant people working in financial services, but they aren't taking home a pay cheque anywhere near as large as that. He's very well connected, one of my friends tells me, and simply connects fund managers to rich friends and relatives of his.

For some reason this news gets to me. At some level, even years after leaving school, I still had the naive belief that even wealthy people had to work extremely hard for their money. Then I step back and see how, if you have a certain amount of wealth, it becomes far, far easier to make much more of it: a gamble on an economic crash here, a flutter on an exit from the European Union there. I think a lot about the anonymity of wealth: how, away from the glare of public scrutiny, the rich quietly acquire vast, unimaginable sums.

The wealthiest kids at school always know where the next wave of money is. I could probably do a decent prediction of global economic trends by simply looking at the degree and first-job choices of some of the boys who leave my school. I remember my surprise when I saw a few of them studying Mandarin for their A-levels; I was struck by what a long-term bet they were making. A couple of years after university, I am added to an email list of old boys from my school, just in case I fancy playing for one of their football teams. I am happy to see the names of friends and acquaintances I haven't seen in a while, but there is something odd about their email addresses – they all have the suffixes of companies I've never seen before. I search for the names of these companies online, and I find that they all have websites with only a couple of pages; a level of discretion which signals that they are places where I can generate immense amounts of money. I do some further research and think, Ah, that makes sense. They are all working at hedge funds. I wonder what the kids who are the most ahead of the curve are studying these days.

THE WEST INDIES APPEARED

One day, when we are both in our mid-thirties, a friend from my time at Eton tells me a story, but first, he asks me a question.

How did I find the racism at school? he enquires. I am curious as to why he is asking. Perhaps, as a white man, he is more likely to have heard racist remarks that people might not utter in my presence. All the same, though, I don't remember all that much prejudice. I think about it. There were a couple of people who were really racist, I say, maybe a few, but not more than that.

He looks amazed; he is appalled that I could have been so oblivious. The racism, he says, was *constant*.

That wasn't my experience, I tell him. There were just a couple of incidents, nothing too bad. Astounded, he gives me an example.

It used to happen whenever they were watching cricket, he says. Seeing the confusion on my face, he quickly explains. Each summer, we used to sit down in the house common room and watch England in the Test matches, he says. And the moment the West Indies appeared on the screen, the racism would start. All the jokes about black people, the stereotypes, all of it.

Oh, I say.

Then I think, Wait, my friend was in the same year as quite a few guys I liked. As I ponder this, he goes on to identify the people who were the worst, the ones who made the most offensive remarks. They are all boys who, at the time, I would have regarded at the very least as good friends.

Really? I say.

Yes.

I imagine the many good times I spent with them, laughing along in some of my happiest moments, and I can't help but feel that so much of that has been shattered. It is a devastating thought, one that hollows me out with sadness. It is no comfort at all to me to think that they probably did not make any of those jokes with me in mind, because to boys like them I was probably the exception that proved the rule: Yes, most black men are big and stupid, but not him: he is different, he is civilised, he is clever. I have learned in the years since that when people's prejudice is so deep-rooted, I don't change their minds about black people; I often just end up confirming their view of the majority. It is a grim reality, and I now only wonder how much time I wasted in their company.

TO GET HOME SAFE

My schoolfriends, the ones I truly trust, introduce me proudly to their partners at their weddings. This guy, says one of them admiringly, is the definition of zero compromise. That praise sticks with me. I never saw myself as a risk-taker – I always thought I was someone who wanted to disappear into the background. But, looking back, I have continually gambled away positions of security for the hope of something more. I could have gone to a local grammar school, but I went to boarding school. After leaving my career as a lawyer, I could have stayed somewhere in the corporate world, perhaps choosing to be a management consultant, but I went and became an artist. It takes this chat with my friend and his fiancée, at the age of thirty-seven, for me to understand who I have always been.

My best friend from school asks me to be the best man at his wedding in Belgium, and it is one of the two or three greatest honours of my entire life. Even though I barely see him these days – we only get to catch up once every two years, as he now runs a brand-design agency in South East Asia – he has chosen me. It means everything to be trusted with such a responsibility – because of my career as an artist, I have often been worried that many people see me as a bit of a joker, someone a little unserious and who never quite grew up, who can't be fully relied upon.

I organise his stag weekend in England on the southern coast, which I arrange promptly and proudly and without incident, and then I am on hand for everything on the Continent the following week.

The wedding is a joy from start to finish. It takes place in a small town just outside the capital, where my best friend's fiancée was brought up, and near a field where an English general – an old boy from my school – won his most famous battle just under 200 years before. The reception is in a beautiful chateau, where I give a speech about my best friend's love for classic cars, and the highlight of the entire event for me is when I walk from the floor, having made my speech, and my best friend's mother rises to hug me as I return to the table. She is thanking me for helping to guide her son through one of the happiest days of his life, and it is a gesture that moves me beyond words.

Maybe I got on with my best friend and his family so well because we had relatively similar backgrounds. We both grew up in small towns in the Thames Valley, and our parents were middle-class professionals: his mother taught children who had special needs; his father worked in brand design and founded the company that they now run together. Sitting there at the wedding, it feels like the end of a journey: one where you grow up so close that you feel a strong sense of responsibility for each other's happiness, no matter how far apart we live or how rarely we are in contact. He will be fine now, I think. He will be fine now.

As I finally relax that evening and the dancing begins, I think back to a point earlier that afternoon, just an hour before the ceremony. My best friend, having shown no nerves until then, was suddenly anxious, and so I went with him to a local supermarket and bought a pocket bottle of whisky, which we sipped in a nearby car park. We then walked around the town while we waited for the church to open its doors, and by the time the wedding official arrived, my best friend was absolutely fine. There's a photo of me from the ceremony that I will always treasure; it's taken about halfway through, perhaps when he and his wife are exchanging their vows, and I am leaning back slightly with the smile of a contented father. My expression reads: *From thirteen years of age to today, I helped him to get home safe.*

WHAT I HAVE TO SAY

I am invited to teach poetry at a school in north-west London and I am nervous about accepting – I am worried that the working-class and mostly black students there might feel that I have nothing to say to them, that they won't be able to relate to someone with my background. Despite my concerns, I say yes, and it is one of the best things I ever do. To my amazement, the children sit there and listen in the assembly, and then later on in the classroom. I tell the teacher who invited me of my shock, and she tells me not to be so surprised, that many of these children don't have fathers at home and so they are keen to hear what I have to say. One of them, a particularly brilliant participant, even asks if I can sign a note as proof that she has actually attended my after-school poetry workshop, since her mother won't believe her otherwise. I am confused – why would her mother doubt that? Later, her teacher tells me that she is normally one of the worst-behaved students in the school. The truth is that I warmed to her at once, a little because she has the same name as my younger sister, and mostly because she reminded me of someone who I provided with a mock entrance interview at university: the same fiercely sharp mind, the fearless intellect. One day, I think, I might like to teach more. Maybe I can make a contribution there.

INTO THE TENDER SUNLIGHT

A couple of years after I leave school, I go back to one of its chapels, where I attend the memorial service for one of its most beloved students. He died in a car accident as his brother drove them both home: a horror that claimed four lives. He was one of the more gifted athletes I have ever known, and far more importantly, one of the kindest souls. In my final year at prep school, in my return to the first eleven, I played alongside him as one of my team's two strikers, scoring fifty-one goals together in twenty-five games. In that partnership he was the chef, while I merely ran around carrying his ingredients.

I still can't believe the brilliance of a free kick that he scored. He took it from the very edge of the area, exactly eighteen yards from goal, and he somehow managed to send the ball soaring over a row of bewildered defenders with such fierce topspin that it landed in the bottom corner of the net. They should have submitted his right foot for scientific tests. By all accounts, he was even better at golf and cricket. I never got to see him play the former sport, but I did get to see him at the crease, his bat shimmering towards the ball with the speed of a hummingbird's wing.

When I look back over the happiest moments of my student life, he frequently turns up in the highlight film. When I played my first match for my prep school, he was the one who produced the moment of genius that led to our victory. I still smile at the time we went on a football tour to Holland, a three-match trip on which we would remain undefeated, and the two of us made a bet. Let's see which one of us will be the first to score on tour, he said, and I assured him that it would be me. We were up against a side from The Hague that day, one of whom bragged loudly before the game, We are coming to defeat you, and I thought, Let's see about that. Our team won the coin-toss and decided to kick off; the whistle went, I passed the ball to my friend, and he surveyed the crowd of opponents ahead of him. They didn't stand a chance.

He drifted past five of them, leaving them strewn about that field like debris after a festival, and just as he entered the area he thrashed a low shot towards goal, which looked set to be one of the best strikes of the season – until the goalkeeper dived down to his left and somehow clawed the ball away, sending it spinning wildly into a nearby patch of mud-clotted grass, where it came to rest directly in my path.

As my friend looked at me aghast, I rolled the ball into the empty net and howled with glee all the way back to my own half, my mischievous grin as wide as the coastline.

We ended up winning that game 12–0, and of course he either created or scored most of the goals, the best player that day by a clear margin. Afterwards, in his presence, I would go on to boast about how I had scored within fifteen seconds of the beginning of a match, shamelessly failing to explain that I had merely profited from his brilliance. He would roll his eyes, but of course he was too good-natured to correct me.

The chapel is full, with attendees having returned from all over the country and beyond, faithfully hearing the call home to grief. The occasion somehow does him justice, because my school is at its very best when honouring its own. It allows our leading rowers to parade triumphantly down the river as we watch from its banks. It celebrates our achievements, not only in newsletters, but also with busts and memorials. It names prizes and local streets after us. It has such a reverence for its students, which continues long after we leave.

There is so much love in every speech that day, and the note of each hymn is summoned from the bottom of all our lungs. At the end of the service, I pass his parents in the doorway, and there is nothing adequate I can say about their wonderful son, but I still try. Then I step outside, into the tender sunlight.

A TAPESTRY OF SADNESS

I am sitting across the table from the boy who bullied me at prep school. I met him a few days earlier, at the memorial service of the friend whom we both knew and loved, and he has asked if he can catch up with me for lunch. It has been so long since the worst things that went between us, and so I agree. The same sunlight from that service has accompanied us for lunch, soothing us through the window that looks out over a vast park in the city. It is not long into our meal before he is apologising to me, and before I am then telling him that he has nothing to say sorry for, and then he is saying no, he is insisting, I must let him apologise. And so I let him say sorry, and the pain tumbles out of him.

Though his stories are not for me to repeat to anyone else, it is quickly clear from listening to him that his fury, at its root, was nothing to do with me. When his volcano erupted, I simply happened to be in the path of the lava. His violence felt so personal towards me, so intimate, but there is a sense in which it could have been anyone. I tell him that I knew this, that at first I thought he hated me, but that after a while I realised that no, I could not have done anything to earn this much rage, and that is what made his attacks hurt less.

As he describes what he has been through, what he has seen, what led him to target me, it sounds as though his life has been a tapestry of sadness. He says that I am one of the few people at prep school who understood him, and I know at once what he means. I have seen untreated trauma like his before, among refugees in our own community, thrashing about everywhere like a rogue fire hose. That's why I could still play next to him in school teams, and sit with him in class, and we could go on to Eton together without further incident, because I knew that he was not yet strong enough to overcome whatever was overwhelming him. I know that he needs to hear that he is forgiven, and so that is what I tell him. I have not seen him since then, but I hope that wherever he is now, whatever he is doing, he has addressed that which was tearing at him, and which at one point threatened to tear me apart.

IRONY

It is only when I am truly happy in a heterosexual relationship that I begin to suspect that I might be homosexual. At first I am bewildered by this realisation. I remember intensely that moment at university: I was walking down a street with my girlfriend of eighteen months when I saw a couple approaching us, and to my alarm I looked at the boy first, not the girl, and my first thought – I couldn't even say it to myself in my head – was that he looked cool, I liked the way he carried himself, because I couldn't yet admit that I found him attractive.

Over the next few months, this awareness only grows, and in my confusion I wonder where it came from. Every account that I read of coming out is from men who say that they always knew, that they always had a mystical sense that they were drawn to the same sex, that it was a veil hanging elegantly over their adolescent lives, just waiting to be drawn back. I cannot relate to that and I am angry because I feel that my future has been hijacked, that everything was going so well. But I know very well what the Bible, such a cornerstone of Ugandan community life, says about homosexuality, and that people like me often risk ending up as outcasts. What would they say back in my parents' country if they knew that I was gay?

Why, I ask myself, is all of this emerging now? I have met someone I love; my degree, though I would much rather be studying something else, is going reasonably well; I have secured a well-paid job at a law firm after graduation. There is no blemish on my reputation, I easily survived my teens, and everything is set for the next stage of my life. Why this, why now?

I tell my girlfriend of my concerns, and that it is best that we stop seeing each other. The effect is devastating. Overnight I lose my best friend and one of the loves of my life, and I am suddenly plunged into a world I do not know or understand. I come out to my friends and family within the year and it takes the best part of a decade before I realise that it is in fact possible to be attracted to both men and women, that it is more accurate to describe myself as bisexual rather than gay, and that this is not the myth that I had been raised to believe. By then I have a different life entirely: I am living in London, having already moved flat five or six times, and I am no longer working in the corporate world, having left shortly after qualifying as a lawyer to pursue my dream of being a writer. I am writing everything I can, from poetry to journalism to song lyrics, I am working for a charity, and it is unusual if I see anyone from school more than once a year. I am now in a very different universe; if not entirely free or at peace, then slowly moving in that direction.

POOR LITTLE POSH BOY

With my fortieth birthday approaching, I decide to go to therapy. My father was forty when he died and so I have always had a silent fear of this age. There is a small part of me that has long believed, irrationally and therefore forcefully, that I won't survive beyond this point, that some grim tragedy will befall me. This age has also long been a milestone for me, because my father achieved so much in the short time that he was alive, and I am not at all sure that I can say the same.

My therapist is a kind man who squints slightly as he listens, as if examining something under a microscope. After a few sessions I am already feeling far better – after changing my perspective, it turns out that I have actually done many things that I can be proud of. But he has noticed something about me, which is that while I am very willing to discuss my race and my bisexuality, I very rarely talk about my time at school.

You just sort of skim over it, he says. I wonder why that is and I eventually conclude that, unlike my race and my sexuality, my class is something that I can choose, and I therefore have no right to complain about it. I chose to go to that school and so I accepted everything that I experienced in that environment, both good and bad.

I brought it on myself, I tell him. It's fine to talk about the challenges of racism and homophobia because those are worthy subjects. But to talk about the issues I have faced just because I went to a boarding school and some of it was tougher than I anticipated? That just feels a bit like *poor little posh boy*.

Poor little posh boy. It's strange how I became that, given how I started out, as one of the smartest kids in the state-school system. I had an entire identity makeover in less than ten years, so I ended up with the accent of a private-school boy and the background of a grammar-school boy but the community of neither. I tell my therapist that maybe that's partly why I moved to Germany, that no one cares so much about that stuff here.

The more I talk about my time at school, the more I realise how much I have to say. It's such a relief to be able to speak. I talk about the guilt, the pressure, the isolation, of being constantly on guard, of the years during school where I thought, So few black boys get to come here – don't blow it, of the many years after school where I thought, So few black boys got to go there – I blew it. And the more I talk, the more I remember who I was all along, not an aspiring financier, simply a writer. I learn to take the good from my school, to discard the bad, and move forwards.

IN EXCELLENT COMPANY

It is not long until my school reunion and I am still not sure if I will go. I mention this to a close relative, and she is nonplussed. Why are you wasting time worrying about that? she says. You've got much bigger things ahead of you. She tells me that whenever I am on the verge of making a decision that feels significant to me, I should not second-guess myself. You are far too strategic a thinker for that, she says.

I don't chat to her for long, but I soon feel much more resolute. For so long I have framed my thoughts in terms of what I have got wrong, in terms of the misuse that I have made of my education. I have never truly looked at myself as someone who has fundamentally taken the right steps. I have so often talked about the cost of my choices, and not so much about how they have borne fruit. I will have to accept that in trying to do what I believe to be the right thing, there will be several months, years even, when I will feel that my work is ineffective. That makes me no different from anyone I have ever admired; in fact, it puts me in excellent company.

So I decide not to go to my school reunion. I am now so far from that world that I no longer own a dinner jacket, an item that was once a staple of my wardrobe; I was once able to fasten a bow tie at the speed of light, but now I find them as odd to handle as a strand of spaghetti. The day of the reunion arrives, and passes, and I feel no regret.

AND THEN BREAKS FREE

A few months later I am back in the UK to see my family for Christmas. It's only a short break, since I want to get back to Germany and work in those few very quiet days just before the new year, to get into a good writing routine for the twelve months ahead. When I get to the airport there is scarcely a queue in the building.

There's still an hour until I board my flight, so I go to a café a few yards from the gates to pick up a coffee and a muffin. As I walk away from the till with my order, I am startled to hear someone call my name; there, ahead of me, is a friend I haven't seen in over two years, since we were last on holiday together in Spain. I was at law school with him, and he now lives about an hour south of London, from where he commutes around Europe to make investments in renewable energy. Today, as our paths cross, he is off to Ireland.

We talk about the recent climate protests and share our relief that at least, at last, a significant number of people are acknowledging the threat of swiftly rising sea levels and man-made climate change. We catch up on family life and football; while I praise the brilliance of the team he supports, he is kind enough not to tease me about the appalling form of mine.

Our flights are boarding just five minutes apart, and there's maybe something a little poignant about how we'll be flying off so soon in entirely different directions. I'll see him soon in the chat group for law-school alumni I've been part of for several years now, and so we take a couple of selfies, just in case its other six members don't believe we've bumped into each other.

I say goodbye to him and sit down at my departure gate. In the seat directly opposite me is a journalist whose writing I greatly admire. After a few minutes I decide to tell him so, and we have a very friendly conversation, despite its grim subject matter, about the current state of our country's politics. We agree on the need for progressive activists and writers to work across borders more than ever before, and he passes me his details in the hope that I will keep in touch.

As I wait for take-off, I reflect upon these two chance meetings, and I consider that, at this point in my life, perhaps I am exactly where I need to be: still writing, still striving. I switch my smartphone to flight mode and put one of my favourite songs on repeat. My plane speeds up, flees the tarmac and then breaks free of the clouds.

ACKNOWLEDGEMENTS

I would like to thank my mother, for giving me everything that she possibly could and then more.

I would also like to thank Rachael Kerr, Katy Guest, DeAndra Lupu and the entire team at Unbound, my agent Abi Fellows at the Good Literary Agency, Miriam, Sarah Maslin Nir, Jennifer Neal, Rhea Schmitt, Ryan Hunn, Joshua Aaron, Lee Davis, Elena Barschazki, Vinay Patel, Nishant Kumar, Nikesh Shukla, Inua Ellams, Soja Subhagar, Amelia Ideh, Jamie McKelvie, Gerdi Bauer, Alex Todorovic, Burcu Güvenç, Jonathan Harding, Jumoké Fashola, Elizabeth Schumacher, Winston Bell-Gam, Anna Winger, The Unicorns and The Council of Good Friends.

A NOTE ON THE AUTHOR

Musa Okwonga is a writer, broadcaster and musician. He has published a collection of poetry and three books about football, including *A Cultured Left Foot*, nominated for the William Hill Sports Book of the Year Award 2008. His work has appeared in *The Good Immigrant* as well as *The Economist*, the *Guardian*, the *Washington Post*, the *Byline Times* and the *New York Times*, among others. He lives in Berlin.

www.okwonga.com

Unbound is the world's first crowdfunding publisher, established in 2011.

We believe that wonderful things can happen when you clear a path for people who share a passion. That's why we've built a platform that brings together readers and authors to crowdfund books they believe in – and give fresh ideas that don't fit the traditional mould the chance they deserve.

This book is in your hands because readers made it possible. Everyone who pledged their support is listed below. Join them by visiting unbound.com and supporting a book today.

A.Nonymous
Marjorie Aaron
Jude Abbott
Maria Abdelmalak
Caritia Abell
Kwojo Ackah
Joshua Adeyemi
Natasha Adom
Folake Adoti-Ryan
Jonathan Aeberhard
Sarah Affenzeller
Samira Ahmed
Corina Ajder
Simon Albert
Lou Aldridge
Puti Naindra Alevia
Pierre Alexander
L Ali
Rupert Alison
Clare Allan
Tom Allason

Rhona Allin
Emma Alter
Lewis Ambrose
Guy Anderson
Josephine Andrews
Bernie Angopa
Paul Ansorge
Raymond Antrobus
Louis Antwi
Gergo Arany
Ursus Arctos
Jon Arnold
Artin Aroutounians
Mandie Atkinson
James Aylett
Joey Ayoub
Wale Azeez
Ikenna Azuike
Tim Bak
Samantha Baloro
Emily Bamford

Yasmina Banaszczuk
Dominic Barker
Anthony Barnett
Rasha Barrage
Justin Barrie
Naomi Baruch
Renée Bauert
Ben Beaton
Laura Beckingham
Harold Bedwei
John Beitter
Emily Bell
Winston Bell-Gam
Belle Benham
Ryan Bestford
Jodi Bickley
Jon Bielby
Ruth Biene
Franziska Bioh
Vegard Bakke Bjerkevik
Abigail Blackburn

Sophie Blacksell Jones
Michael Blesic
Steve Bloomfield
Gene Bogolepov
JJ Bola
Nitya Boora
Oliver Boothroyd
Clarissa v. Bormann
Pete Boschini
Elijah Bossa
Julio Bouza
Marc Boxser
Andreas Brandis
David Braneck
Kelly Brantner
Virginia Braun
Corrie Bray
Richard W H Bray
Annie Brechin
Andy Brereton
Lesley-Anne Brewis
Emma Bridge
Ciara Briggs
Frederick Bristol
Peter Broad
Ross Brockman
Kristian Brodie
Clare Bromfield
Russell Brooks
Jeff Brown
Josh Brown
Lewis Brown
Symeon Brown
Johanna Brownell
David Bruce
Richard Budgey
Joe Burrows
James Butler
Season Butler

Stuart Butler
Imogen Butler-Cole
Kester Byass
Katie Byford
Conor Byrne
Janet Cadsawan
Vid Calovski
Rupert Candy
Phi Tan Cao
Nic Carey
Jared Carnie
Ann Carrier
Jordan Cartmell
Spencer Castello
David Castle
Anu Chahal
Oliver Chamberlain
Manrouf Chanfi
Hsintao Chang
Hugo Chapman
Tom Chatfield
Niki Cheong
Darren Chetty
Lumiere Chieh
Sandeep Chohan
Kyo Choi
Vera Chok
Kate Church
Ben Clarke
Megan Clement
Mary Ann Clements
Charlie Clover
Avery Cobb
Alex Cobham
John Coldham
Alex Cole
Chris Cole
Anastasia Colman
C Connellan

Suzanne Connelly
Chris Cook
Simon Cook
Zoe Cooper
Joe Corcoran
Martin Cordiner
Anita Coulson
Barbara Cox
James Cox
John Crawford
Ross Crooke
Steve Cunningham
Fernanda Cury Cabral
Chris D'Souza
Alex Dale
Helen Dallimore
Daniel Daly
Wasi Daniju
Shameel Danish
Ki Dara
Daniellè Dash
Rishi Dastidar
Divya Dattani
Owen Davies
Michele Davis
Antonia Davis-Maxwell
Natalia Davydova
David De Felipe Mesquida
Lianne de Mello
Gervase de Wilde
Jon Dean
Margaret Decker
Max'ed Deeq
John DeGraft-Johnson
Fatima del Carmen Lopez
	Sevilla
Ed Dennehy
Tobias Denskus
Joe Derry Hall

Ashwin Desikan
David Devlin
Richard Diffenthal
Maggie Dodson
Ben Donovan
Jairo Dorado Cadilla
Kathrin Dornheim
Colin Douglas
Tiernan Douieb
Cressida Downing
Fintan Dudleston
Heike Duerr
Charles Dunst
Charlie Dupré
Ankit Dutta
Natasha Dyer-Williams
Ben Dzialdowski
Robert Eardley
Rob Edgerton
Rachel Edwards
Cameron Eide
Catriona Eilidh
Aniefiok 'Neef' Ekpoudom
Ismail El Kadiri
Rudi Eliott Lockhart
Shannon Elizabeth
Ellie Elliott
Michael Ellis
Annemarie Elsom
Calvin Embling
Trinka Endaya
Lisa English
Leila Essa
Jake Evans
Will Evans
Bernardine Evaristo
Olivia Everett
Rambaut Fairley
Jumoké Fashola

Kemi Fatoba
Delphine Favier
Luis Félix
Abi Fellows
Serdar Ferit
Susannah Field
Jess Fleming
Molly Fletcher
Edward Flood
Decorsey Folkes
Mark Forsyth
Daniel Foster
Edward Foulds
Liam Francis
Richard Francis
Edith Franconi
Peter Fraser
Trista Winnie Fraser
Mary Freer
Bridget Frost
Jo Fry
Yara Pascale Füssel
Elaine Gallacher
Dan Ganderton
Bryan Garcia
Christine Garcia
Heidi Gardner
Jess Gastaud
Jeremy Gavron
Clara Gay
Claire Genevieve
Brandi Geurkink
Divya Ghelani
Anindita Ghosh
Ashoke Ghosh
Daniele Gibney
Josh Gilham
Aly Gillani
Vicky Gillard

Kieron Gillen
Helen Gimber
Joe Gitter
Ollie Glanvill
Vicki Gloak
Lou Glover
Fabien Goa
Max Godsland
Zack Goldman
Miles Gould
Joel Grace Fisher
Andrew Granato
Eugene Grant
Sarah Grant
Augustus Gray
Alexander Greene
Matt Greene
Kyle Greenwood
Hannah Grünewald
Katy Guest
Shobna Gulati
Guy Gunaratne
Gabi Hagenberger
Olivia Hagger
Emily Hames
Niki Hanbuch
Will Hancox
David Hanna
Hannah and Tom
Anna Hannu
Donna Hardcastle
Jonathan Harding
Josh Harding
Stephen Hardman
Samuel Harker
Taylor Harper
Becca Harper-Day
Daniel Harris
Shelley Harris

The Harris Hess family
Matt Harrison
A.F. Harrold
Laurie Hartley
Liz Harvey-Kattou
Zakir Hasan
Lucy Haskell
Tim Hassall
Suridh Hassan
Sarah Hawk
Tara Hawk
Tom Hay
James Heale
@HeardinLondon
Rachel Henderson
Ronan Hennessy
Sam Herbert
Megan Hession
Tessa Hetherington
Lara Hewitt
Machel Hewitt
Christopher Hill
Lewis Hill
John Hitchin
Matt Hoban
Jennifer Hobson
Ben Hodgson
Chris Hodgson
Al Hogarth
James Holden
Sj Holgate
Iain Hollingshead
Ollie Holt
David Hopkins
Kyle Hudspeth
Felix Huesmann
Jay Humphrey
Ryan Hunn
Jeremy Hutchison

Lizzie Huxley-Jones
Josh Hyams
Samir Ibrahim
Amelia Ideh
Tom Impallomeni
Eilidh Innes
Lois Ireson
Calum Jacobs
Leah James
Louise James
Mike James
Billy Jarvis
Eresha Jayatillake
Anna Jeevanjee
Garan Jenkin
Rodric Jenkin
Lisa Jenkins
Stephen K. Jenkins
Mandy Jenkinson
Nico Jersch
Annelise Jespersen
Lucas Johnson
Lizzy Johnstone
Eric Jones
Hannah Jones
Pete Jones
Sophie Jones
Kevin Jussel
Manveer S Kahlon
Jeegar Kakkad
Rohan Kallicharan
Wei Ming Kam
Ryu Kawashima
Andrej Kelemen
Luke Kemp
Christina Kennedy
Saskia Kersten
Vicky Kett
Ali Khan

Haroon Khan
Mishaal Khan
Dan Kieran
Kui Kihoro Mackay
Atim Kilama
Patrick King
Jackie Kirkham
Vanessa Kisuule
Amy Kittelstrom
Rosie Knight
Will Knight
Lukas Knöfler
Daniel Kolodziej
Sarathy Korwar
Hendryk Korzeniowski
Carina Krause
Lolita Laguna Crespo
Julian Land
Ruth Landrigan
Rupert Lang
Emma Laxton
Sang Lee
Sunyoung Lee
Diane Leedham
Emilia Leese
Philip Levine
Chantelle Lewis
Maissa Lihedheb
Catherine Lindo
Ben Lindsay
Rob Lingo
Rob Linham
Juliet Litman
Mascha Litterscheid
Catherine Little
LJ
Benedict Lloyd-Jones
Andrew Lockett
Natasha Lomboy

Victoria Long
Laura-Ioana Luca
Remy Lupica
Mayo Lynette
Sophia MacBlain
Alan Macdonald
Tom Mackay
Cait MacPhee
John Madden
Sean Magee
Sandeep Mahal
Mateja Maher
Shaun Maher
Marija Maher Diffenthal
Gita Malhotra
Jessica Malone
Gowtham Reddy Manda
Wendy Mann
Annie Mark-Westfall
David Marriott
Tim Marston
Alex Marten
SR Martin
Melissa Martorell Luque
Dara Matiluko
Harry Matthews
Mike Matthews
Linda Maynard
Chonai Mbirimi
Kirsten McAteer
Janice McCombie
Louise McCudden
Matt McGinn
Jayne McGlynn
Eusebius Mckaiser
Jamie McKelvie
Martin McLaughlin
Stuart McLean
Brian Mcleish

Conor Meade
Isabelle Meli
Joe Melia
Eliav Mengem
Jacky Mercey
Nick Metler
Ryn Miake-Lye
Fergus Midforth
Emerson Milford Dickson
Emili Milinković-Stevenson
Roger Miller
Andrew Milne
Saima Mir
Chris Mitchell
Eoghan Mitchell
John Mitchinson
Richard Mkoloma
Lucy Moffatt
James Mohide
Kevin Molloy
Maxine Monu
Ann Morgan
Angela Morton
Manos Moschopoulos
Nadia Motraghi
Theodore Moyo
Ashish Mudaliar
Ted Mulcauley
Mike Murphy
Kay Murray
Gil Myers
Udi Nachmany
Erum Naqvi
Carlo Navato
Jennifer Neal
Pierre Nedd
Conor Nevins
Rich Newbold
Josh Newiss

Rachel Newman
Jai Newton
Julian Ngai
Archie Nhlangano
Sarah Nir
Trevor Norris
Barry Norton
Helen L Norton
Kimberley Nyamhondera
Kaley O'Hara
David O'Riordan
Lizzy O'Shea
Ros O'Sullivan
Fearghal O'Loan
Mic Oala
Emma Obanye
Michael Obi
MoyinOluwa Odugbemi
Okell Ojara
Kelechi Okafor
Taiwo Oke
Kwesi Okutu
Damon Oldcorn
Emily Oram
Andrey Orr
Anna Orr
Stephen Orr
Majdi Osman
Sarah Osman
Gabrielle Osrin
Daniela Othieno
Faraaz Outim
Laura Ovenden
Nic Owen
Derek Owusu
Stuart Page
Manjiri Palicha
Camilla Marie Pallesen
Nii Ayikwei Parkes

Nic Parsons	Liam Read	Vijay Sapre
Dan Partovi	Aruba Red	Rhea Schmitt
Alison Partridge	Graham Rehling	Karolin Schnoor
Brieann Pasko	Caroline Reid	Charlott Schönwetter
Sufiya Patel	Wil Reidie	Robert Schulze
Vinay Patel	Phil Reynolds	Elizabeth Schumacher
Michael Pavey	Sarah Riccomini	Tilo Schumann
Jo Pearson	Jane Richardson	Pia Schuschies
Shehan Peiris	Jennifer Richardson	Jasmina Schweimler
Henry Pelly	Darren Richman	Paul Scraton
Elaine Penrose	Ian Ridley	Matt Scroggins
John Perkins	Liam Riley	Jess Search
Hugo Perks	Norman Riley	Leon Seremelis
Bob Perna	Matt Rivers	Mark Ivan Serunjogi
Azadê Peşmen	Jacqueline Roach	Hari Sethi
Anthony Peter	Eve Roberts	Zain Shaikh
Sarah Peter	Neil Roberts	John Shale
Olivia Phipps	Sean Roberts	Samantha Shannon
Aisha Phoenix	Tony Roberts	Abbi Shaw
Dave Pickering	Imogen Robertson	Jessica Shea
Scroobius Pip	John Robinson	Sean Sheehy
Kevin Pocock	Richard Robinson	Alexander Shields
Polarbear	Vitty & Richard Robinson	Adam Shingleton
Justin Pollard	Deanna Rodger	Haroon Shirwani
Beki Pope	Scott Rogers	Christopher Shoop-Worrall
Tayo Popoola	Pippa Rogerson	Francesca A Shrapnel
Tania Porteous	Romavia	Nikesh Shukla
Andrew Powell	Kinga Rona	Amardeep Sian
Bert Preece	Will Rose	Miguel Sicart
James Pryor	Fenella Rouse	Beth Silver
Laura Quin	David Rudin	Maja Sinn
Susi Quinn	Archie Ruggles-Brise	Ashley Skilton
Sadiah Qureshi	Sheila Ruiz	Chris Slade
Penny Rabiger	Alistair Rush	Hazel Slavin
Giles Radford	Gisele Salazar	Joshua Slingsby
Harold Raitt	Justin Salhani	Andy Sloan
Matthew Ramirez	Ravin Sampat	Maria Slovakova
Polly Randall	Christoph Sander	Angela Smith
Cat Randle	Chris Santos	Daryl Snow

Ana Sobral	Tommy Torkar	Christina Wheeler
Koyeli Solanki	Alison Torrens	Simon White
Will Sorrell	Christopher Trent	Brian Whitehead
Philip Spedding	Joe Tuck	Edith Whitehead
Joe Spence	Neville Tumulty	Alex Whitmore
Greg Spiro	Ryan Turnbull	Liz Wigley
Ceylan Stafford-Bloor	Luke Turner	Claire Wilby
Jess Stalley	Mike Turner	Louise Wilkin
John Stawpert	Jo Unwin	Kate Wilkinson
Susie Steed	Anouschka Urrejola	David Willbe
Cathryn Steele	Clara Usiskin	Julius Williams III
Eleni Stefanou	Julia Utiger	Martin Willis
Dafna Steinberg	Eva van Gerven	Charlie Wilson
Alistair Stewart	Sofia Vester	Dan Wilson
John Stokoe	Tom Victor	Johanna Wilson
Allison Strachan	Kate Vines	Mathew Wilson
Kay Stratton	Ryu Voelkel	Alex Winter
Faith Stringer	Saskia Vogel	Lucie Winter
Lynn Svensson	Sebastian Vollnhals	Naomi Woddis
James Swyer	Khin Voong	Gretchen Woelfle
Kirsty Syder	Donan Vye	Ian Woodbyrne
Vinay Talwar	Camilla Waite	Andrea Woodhouse
Lisa Taner	Richard Walton	Funmi Worrell
Daniel Tatarsky	Daniel Ward	Stephen Wright
Oni Tate	Ruth Warham-Smith	Timothy Wright
Ben Taylor	Anna Warrington	Alfonso Yap
Jeremy Taylor	Aisha Washington	James Yates
Rob Taylor	Belinda Washington	Henry Yorke
Ruth Taylor	Dickon Waterfield	Neil Young
Jo Tedds	Andrew Waters	Simon Young
Teddy	Ruth Waterton	Abby Young-Powell
Jazz Tehara	Benjamin Weber	Jose Yumet
Adizah Tejani	Mandy Weber	Helen Zaltzman
Matty Thavenot	Claire E. Webster	João Zamith
Rajesh Thind	Georgie Weedon	Verónica Zaragovia
Fraser Thomas	Shawn Westcott	Elisa Zenck
Frank Thomson	Tom Westwood	Andreas Zuber
Bec Tigue	Revd R. P. Whaite	
Ruth Till	Daniel Whalen	